POEMS AND
RHYMED PRAYERS

T0265982

POEMS AND
RHYMED PRAYERS

Eberhard & Emmy Arnold
Else von Hollander

THE PLOUGH PUBLISHING HOUSE

08 07 06 05 04 03   8 7 6 5 4 3 2 1

Front Cover Art: Ralf Blumenstein

ISBN: 0-87486-928-5

Acknowledgments

This book was prepared for July 26, 2003, the 120th anniversary of
Eberhard Arnold's birth. Many people were involved in the process –
collecting, cataloging, typing, translating, and editing – but special thanks
are due the following brothers and sisters: Eileen Robertshaw, Hugo
Brinkmann, Marianne Zimmermann, Lotti Magee, Derek Wardle, Hela
Ehrlich, Miriam Potts, and Mary Ann Sayvetz.

Printed in the USA

Contents

Translator's Note

Aside from Eberhard's poems to Emmy in the *Brautbriefe* ("bridal letters"), most of his originals were lost in the Carriage House fire at Woodcrest in 1957. Fortunately, numerous copies made by Emmy, Annemarie, Hardy and Edith, and other family members survive; they are the basis for this collection. Variations and discrepancies were solved by following the most common version, or Eberhard's own revisions in typed collections prepared in 1934–1935.

At least a dozen of Eberhard's poems were set to music in Sannerz and published in *Sonnenlieder* (1924). In the 1960s and 1970s, about fifty more were translated into English at Woodcrest, and made into songs; most appeared in *Songs of Light* (1977). Almost all of these poems have been revised (in some cases completely retranslated) for this collection. See the note on page 351.

As regards the title of this book, it comes from Emmy, who said of her husband's poems, "Many are really rhymed prayers."

Introduction

December 1935 was cold and wet and depressing at the Rhön Bruderhof. The brotherhood was still reeling from the recent loss of Eberhard Arnold, their "Word Leader." Debts were mounting, and food and fuel were in short supply. Internal struggles had weakened the resolve of many, and outwardly, too, the circle limped along, most of the able-bodied men having fled the country to avoid conscription into Hitler's army. Nazis and nosy neighbors spied constantly on the community, and there was a lingering sense of dread in the air.

But all was not gloom and doom. In a letter she wrote to a friend in England the same month, Edna Percival, a guest at the Rhön, spoke with optimism of how the Bruderhof would not give up:

> The wonderful thing is that for us Eberhard can never die. In all his poems and songs, which we use almost daily, the essence of everything he lived is expressed, and stands for all time.

This book is the most complete collection of those poems to date, many of them in English for the first time. Writing about the earliest ones, Eberhard's eldest son, Hardy, explained:

They stem from the time when, as a student, my father was involved in the Salvation Army [1903–1904] and the German Christian Student Union [1905–1906] mainly in Halle, Breslau, and Erlangen. They are about repentance and conversion, and a burning love for Jesus. They speak of discipleship and struggle, the outpouring of the Spirit, and the coming into being of a true *Gemeinde* – not a church or sect, but a consecrated body. They also voice jubilant praise and thanks to God. They are imbued with a fiery spirit.

So are the "engagement poems" of 1907–1909, which follow. The outpourings of a young man so passionately in love that he begged his fiancée to write to him "at least once a day," they are emotionally charged. But they are not conventional love poems. Almost all end by pointing their recipient (and by extension, every reader) toward Christ.

Eberhard wrote numerous essays, but almost no poems, from 1910 to 1920. After marrying on December 20, 1909, he and Emmy raised a family of five and moved from one place to another: Halle, Leipzig, the Tirol, and finally Berlin. There, as literary director of the Furche Publishing House, he acquired and edited books, contributed regularly to several periodicals, and kept up a demanding schedule of public lectures and "open evenings" for discussion and debate.

1920, a watershed year, saw the Arnolds abandon the security of the Berlin suburbs for a life of unknowns in the village of Sannerz, where they embarked on what Eberhard called an "adventure of faith" – a life of voluntary poverty and community. By 1921, he was writing poems again. Many mirror the struggles of the fledgling circle: their search for unity in the middle of discord; their insistence on genuineness in an era of crumbling formalities; their desire for silence amid upheaval and noise. Many express joy – in music and color, in circling dancers and orbiting stars. But there are also echoes of what Eberhard met in the cities where his speaking engagements took him: the disillusionment of a generation whose youth was overshadowed by Germany's crushing defeat at the end of World War I, a growing dissatisfaction with tradition, a disgust for religious hypocrisy, and a bewildering jumble of new political ideas.

Summarizing the poems from the next period, the last decade of his father's life, Hardy notes that they

> have their root in the struggles and victories of the communal life at Sannerz and the Rhön. They are mainly about the breaking in of God's kingdom of justice on earth, and the ongoing struggle between light and darkness, which takes place in every heart.

He identifies other themes as well: the presence of God in nature, the bankruptcy of the existing social order, the necessity of personal rebirth, and the importance of mission.

Eberhard's poems cover a broad spectrum, from the unabashed evangelistic fervor of "When, O when" to the expressionistic imagery of "All is silent"; from the sophistication of "Cliffs are clamoring" to the utter simplicity of "It is finished." But no matter their style, they all glow with the same deep conviction.

The poems of Emmy Arnold, Eberhard's wife (and widow for forty-five long years) need no introduction. They were one as few couples are. Even before they knew each other, they were searching for answers to the same questions and being led toward the same common cause. After Eberhard's death at the age of fifty-two, Emmy fought on toward his life's goal – a truly Christ-centered community – even as others lost that vision and in some cases derided it.

The poems of Emmy's sister Else von Hollander are self-explanatory too. Sharing the Arnolds' faith from 1907 on (and spurring them on at several junctures, as when she received baptism) she moved in with them in 1913 and never left. Eberhard's valued assistant in his publishing work, she was Emmy's right hand, too, and closest confidante. In 1920, she was the first to join them after they burned their bridges in Berlin and moved to Sannerz. Her bequest, to quote Markus Baum, was a "steadfast and boundless confidence in the course they pioneered."

Eberhard's younger sister Hannah once said of her brother that his faith was "a joyful, victorious Christianity that had its roots in the certainty of forgiveness of sins." As for his zeal in sharing it, she said, "There was no one who was safe from him, no one whom he would not confront with the commands of Jesus, and the need to decide for or against him." If this book confronts even one reader with the same, it will have served its purpose.

May 2003

Eberhard

Voran zum Sieg!

Wir scharen uns zum heil'gen Streit
in Gottes Kraft zusammen!
Der Herr macht uns zum Kampf bereit,
schenkt uns des Geistes Flammen!
Denn was uns treibt zu Sieg und Schlacht,
hat Gottes Geist in uns entfacht.
Preis ihm! O halleluja!

Im Herrn ist unsre Kraft allein,
er führt uns treu zum Siege!
Ihm müssen wir die Kräfte weihn,
dass Satan unterliege!
Denn brechen wir des Feindes Macht,
so hat der Herr den Sieg vollbracht.
Preis ihm! O halleluja!

So soll uns stets des Geistes Glut
zu neuem Kampf entflammen,
zu immer neuem, kühnen Mut
die Kämpfer führn zusammen,
dass wir, gefüllt mit Gottes Macht,
den Feind besiegen in der Schlacht!
Preis ihm! O halleluja!

Gott hat erfüllet unsre Brust
mit lauter Siegesfreude,

In 1899, at sixteen, Eberhard experienced a life-changing conversion. As his early poems show, however, he was just as concerned with the salvation of those around him. At first forming a small Bible study group with fellow high school stu-

On to victory!

We've gathered for the holy fight
in the power of God's name.
He makes us fit for battle,
gives us the Spirit's holy flame.
The Spirit rouses heart and soul
and drives us on toward his goal,
so praise him: Hallelujah!

Our hope is in the Lord alone,
who leads to victory at length.
And thus, to overcome the Foe,
to God we must give all our strength.
For when we vanquish Satan's might,
the Lord himself has won the fight,
so praise him: Hallelujah!

The Spirit shall ignite our zeal
for each new battle with his fire
and draw together all who fight,
and fan their flames of courage higher.
Thus shall we slay the Enemy,
armed by the Lord for victory,
so praise him: Hallelujah!

God fills us with triumphant joy,
for boundless victory is ours.

dents, he soon became involved with the Salvation Army,
whom he had long admired. By 1903 he was speaking at their
meetings, distributing their newspaper, and even preaching in
the streets.

EBERHARD ARNOLD

dass wir dem Feind mit heil'ger Lust
entreissen seine Beute.
So streiten wir bis an den Tod
und bleiben treu in jeder Not!
Preis ihm! O Halleluja!

Breslau, 26. Februar 1903

Wie hat dein Jesus dich geliebt!
Für dich am Kreuz er starb.
Er ist's, der dir Vergebung gibt,
der längst um dich schon warb!

Refrain:
O Sünder, Sünder, komm noch heut
zum Heiland Jesus Christ!
Er ist so willig und bereit,
dass du ganz glücklich bist!

Du weisst, dass dir der Friede fehlt
und dass dein Herz beschwert.
Du hast die Hölle dir gewählt,
weil dir die Sünde wert!

Warum willst du noch zögern heut,
warum nicht kommen gleich?
Des Heilands Hände sind bereit!
Er will dich machen reich!

Breslau, Februar 1903

He lets us snatch the devil's prey
to safety from hell's evil powers.
So we shall stand and fight till death,
steadfast and loyal to our last breath,
and praise him: Hallelujah!

Breslau, February 26, 1903

How Jesus loves you! For your sake
he died upon the cross.
He will forgive you, for he sought
you when you were still lost.

Refrain:
> O sinner, come to Christ today.
> He'll save you from distress.
> He wants to bless you here and now
> with perfect happiness.

You know that you can find no peace.
Your heart is weighted down.
But it was you who chose this hell,
to sin were gladly bound.

Why do you linger, holding back?
Should you not rather haste?
He waits for you with open arms
to make you richly blest.

Breslau, February 1903

Aus dem Herzen zu Gott

Wann kommt die Stunde, in der ich werd' rein,
    rein, ach ganz rein?
Möcht' durch das Blut ganz heilig gern sein,
    rein, ach ganz rein.
Oh, all die Sünde aus Schwachheit macht
Schmerz,
laut nach der Heiligung schreiet mein Herz,
sendet voll Sehnen den Ruf himmelwärts!
    Rein, ach ganz rein!

O lieber Heiland, so wasche mich heut,
    rein, ach ganz rein!
Mache mein Herz für's Göttliche weit,
    rein, ach ganz rein!
Gib mir die brennende Liebe zum Herrn,
die auch das Schwerste tut freudig und gern.
Mache mein Leben zum leuchtenden Stern!
    Rein, ach ganz rein!

Jesus erhört dich und macht dich jetzt rein,
    rein, ja ganz rein!
Heut durch das Blut kannst heilig du sein,
    rein, ja ganz rein!
Leg dich zu Füssen dem Heiland jetzt hin,

Remembering her father speaking at open-air revival meet-ings on the Dölauer Heide (near Halle) in 1914, Eberhard's old-est daughter Emi-Margret writes (1980): "Sometimes Papa suggested songs he himself had written. He would read out a verse, and then everyone would sing it to a well-known tune, and then he would have it repeated with variations: 'Once

From my heart to God

When, O when, will my heart be made
    pure, truly pure?
Would by his blood that I could be
    pure, truly pure!
How I am pained by weakness and sin,
how my heart cries to be holy within!
Filled with great longing I shout to heaven:
    pure, make me pure!

Wash me clean, dear Savior, today:
    clean, truly clean!
Open my heart to your will, I pray –
    clean, truly clean!
Give me a strong, burning love to the Lord,
love that rejoices to do what is hard.
Lord, make my life shine for you like a star:
    make it truly clean!

Jesus will cleanse you; he's heard your plea:
    pure, truly pure!
Saved through his blood today you can be
    pure, truly pure!
Cast yourself down at the feet of your king,

more! Now just the men! Now the women! Now all to-gether!'" About this particular song, Emi-Margret writes, "The last verse especially was sung again and again. We did not sing this song in later years, but it made a deep impression on me. I wanted so badly to be completely pure, and again and again something happened that spoiled this."

ruf heut im Glauben mit freudigem Sinn:
Heilig, ja heilig aus Gnaden ich bin,
 rein, ja ganz rein!

Breslau, März 1903

Gebet

O Jesu, Heiland, was ich habe,
das gebe ich dir alles gern,
und diese kleine, schwache Gabe
wird kraftvoll in der Hand des Herrn.

Refrain:
 O Jesu, komm mit deinem Segen!
 Beleb dein Werk in dieser Stadt!
 Lass froh im Geist sich jeden regen,
 der deine Gnad' erfahren hat!

O Jesu, Heiland, was ich brauche,
das ist dein Geist mit seiner Kraft!
Berühre mich mit deinem Hauche,
der immer neues Leben schafft!

O Jesu, Heiland, was dir fehlet,
ist eine ganz geweihte Schar,
die keine Sündenmacht mehr quälet,
die dir gehorsam, frei und wahr.

In April 1905, Eberhard began his studies at Breslau, where
he found others who shared his zeal for Jesus. Their meeting

shout out in faith, and triumphantly sing.
You shall be made, by sheer grace, through him,
   pure, truly pure!

Breslau, March 1903

Prayer

All that I have, my Lord and Savior,
I bring to thee freewillingly.
It will – although a feeble offering –
gain new strength and worth in thee.

Refrain:
   O Jesus, enter with thy blessing,
   revive thy work here in this place.
   Let every soul awake with joy
   and know the power of thy grace.

O Jesus, Savior, how I long
to breathe from thine own mighty breath!
Touch me with thy spirit. Give me
life anew: save me from death.

What thou lack'st, Lord, is a people
consecrated to thy name –
a people truthful and obedient,
a people free from guilt and shame.

place – and his spiritual home for the next two years – was
the local chapter of the German Christian Student Union.

So gib den Geist, der uns erneuet,
der von uns nimmt, was dich betrübt,
dass wir nichts tun, was uns reuet,
aus Lieb' zu dem, der uns geliebt.

Send uns die Kraft, mit der erfüllet
wir siegen über jeden Feind,
die Kraft, die jeden Kummer stillet
und tröstet jedes Herz, das weint.

Breslau, ca. Mai 1905

Jesus, mein Alles

O mein Herr Jesu, wenn ich dein nicht wäre,
noch immer suchte meine eigne Ehre,
wie traurig wäre dann mein armes Leben,
Satan ergeben.

Ja, mein Herr Jesu, wenn's deine Kraft nicht gäbe,
die mich errettete, dass ich nun lebe,
so müsste ich des Todes friedlos sterben,
ewig verderben.

O halleluja! Gottes Liebe rettet!
Und wenn ihr noch so viele Sünden hättet,
die Liebe Gottes will euch dennoch geben
ewiges Leben.

Drum, mein Herr Jesu, will ich alles lassen,
um einzig deine teure Hand zu fassen,

Take from us what saddens thee,
renew our spirits, quench our thirst.
Keep us from deeds we'll later rue,
for love of thee, who loved us first.

Give us strength that we may conquer
all our foes – give victories,
and strength to quiet every sorrow.
Comfort every heart that grieves.

Breslau, ca. May 1905

Jesus, my all in all

If I were not your own, O Jesus, Savior,
but stood apart, insistent on my honor,
I'd soon be lost, by wretchedness maligned,
to Satan consigned.

Yes, Jesus, if I were bereft and empty
of your power, which gave me life and saved me,
I'd face death's door without the peace you lend –
eternally condemned.

Praise God for his great love, which brings
    redemption,
forgives and cleanses all, without exception!
In his great love he gives, in place of strife,
everlasting life.

Hence will I every other force withstand
except your call, and take your loving hand.

will stets auf deines Blutes Kraft vertrauen,
auf dich nur bauen.

Breslau, ca. Mai 1905

Jesus, meine Zuflucht

In dir, O Herr, ist meine Stärke!
In mir ist alle Kraft dahin.
Von nirgends ich noch Hilfe merke,
nach dir alleine steht mein Sinn!

Nach dir, O Herr, steht mein Verlangen,
wenn alles andre um mich bricht.
Doch deine Arme mich umfangen.
Ja, deine Liebe lässt mich nicht.

In dir, O Herr, ist volle Gnade,
auf dich vertrau' ich felsenfest.
Du führst mich, Jesus, stets gerade,
wenn meine Hand dich nur nicht lässt.

So bleib' ich treu auf deinem Wege,
den du mir selbst gewiesen hast.
In deine Hand ich alles lege
und werf' auf dich die ganze Last!

Breslau, 30. Juli 1905

In your blood's power I'll trust eternally
and build on thee.

Breslau, ca. May 1905

Jesus, my refuge

In thee, O Lord, I find new power
when my own power is spent and gone.
I see help coming from nowhere else,
to thee alone in hope I turn.

For thee, Lord, I reach out in longing,
though all around me breaks and falls.
Thy arms shall hold me safe forever;
thy love remains, whatever befalls.

In thee, O Lord, is grace abundant.
On thee I trust as on a rock.
The way thou lead'st me on is straight,
my hand in thy firm hand is locked.

So I shall keep, steadfast and faithful,
upon the path that thou hast shown.
Into thy hands I lay my burdens,
entrust all things to thee alone.

Breslau, July 30, 1905

Jesus, meine Stärke

O mein teurer, starker Heiland,
gib mir deines Geistes Kraft!
Gib, dass niemals so wie weiland
eine Kluft im Leben klafft
zwischen deinen Wahrheitsworten
und dem, was ich tu' und sag'!
Gib Gehorsam hier und dorten,
dass in dir ich alles wag!

O du mächtiger Erlöser,
lass an dir mich hangen fest!
Wird der Feind auch ernster, böser,
deine Hand mich doch nicht lässt!
Dir vertrauen, das heisst siegen,
auf dich bauen in der Not.
Keiner Macht kann unterliegen
wer vertraut bis in den Tod!

Breslau, Juli 1905

Jesus, mein Licht

Mein Auge sieht so trübe,
mein Herz ist so beschwert;
nichts, nichts als deine Liebe
ist mir als Trost noch wert.
So hilf mir denn zum Frieden,
mein teurer Herzensfreund,

Jesus, my strength

Hear me, strong, belovéd Savior,
give thy spirit's strength to me.
Grant that while I live I never
fall again so far from thee
that a gaping chasm yawns
between thy true word and my deeds.
Rather, in thee daring all things,
let me serve obediently.

Hear me, strong Redeemer, let me
hold to thee eternally.
Though the Enemy grow fiercer,
thou wilt not let go of me.
No matter what my need, I'll build
on thee, for faith means victory.
No force can overcome the one
who, unto death, still trusts in thee.

Breslau, July 1905

Jesus, my light

My sight is dim and clouded;
my heavy heart, weighed down.
Nothing can give me comfort
except thy love alone.
And so I beg thee, my heart's friend:
such peace on me bestow

dass nichts mir nimmt hienieden
die Sonne, die mir scheint.

O Jesu, du alleine
bist meines Herzens Licht;
bei dieses Lichtes Scheine
stört alles andre nicht.
Dir will ich froh vertrauen,
in dir ist meine Kraft.
Auf dich nur will ich bauen
als den, der Wunder schafft.

Breslau, Juli 1905

Golgatha

O mein Heiland, Lob und Ehre
sei dir allein in Ewigkeit!
Dein Ruhm sich täglich, stündlich mehre!
Er gehe wie die Welt so weit!

O Herr Jesu, meine Worte,
sie sagen es nicht laut genug,
was mir geschah an jenem Orte,
an dem ich selbst dir Wunden schlug!

Ja, nur Golgatha alleine
soll Tag für Tag mein alles sein.
So oft Vergangnes ich beweine,
erquicket mich des Kreuzes Schein!

Und wenn Sünde mich versuchet,
denk' ich ans Kreuz mit seiner Kraft.

that nothing ever cloud the sun
that shines on me, below.

O Jesus, Savior, thou alone
art my heart's light and joy.
Nothing can thy brightness
ever hinder or destroy.
And I shall trust thee gladly –
for my strength comes from thee –
and build my life on thee alone,
who worketh wondrously.

Breslau, July 1905

Golgotha

May honor and praise be thine alone,
O Savior mine, eternally.
May, hour by hour, thy glory grow
until the whole world knows of thee!

Lord Jesus, how I wish I had
the voice to fittingly proclaim
aloud the grace of Golgotha,
where for my sins you bore all blame.

Yes, what took place there on the cross
shall be forever in my sight.
And when I brood on past regrets
I shall be quickened by its light.

And when temptations plague my heart
(though I have long since died with thee)

Ich bin gestorben längst mit Jesus,
der Satansmacht dahingerafft.

Was auch komme, Ruhm und Schande,
mein Ich starb dort am Kreuzesstamm.
Ich sag' es laut in alle Lande,
es starb für mich das Gotteslamm!

So kann ich heute in ihm leben,
an ihm nur hangen ganz allein.
Und wie der Weinstock dort den Reben,
ist mir der Herr mein ganzes Sein.

Breslau, 17. Oktober 1905

Sein Blut

Mein lieber Jesu, sei gepriesen
für deines Geistes Feuerkraft,
die mich ans Kreuz und Blut gewiesen,
wo Gott ein völlig Neues schafft!

Das Blut am Kreuz, es sei gelobet,
dass es vertilgt der Sünde Macht!
Denn was auch alles ringsum tobet,
im Blick aufs Kreuz man kämpft und wacht!

Im Blick aufs Kreuz muss jeder siegen,
denn dort ist alles abgetan!

On June 12, 1907, in a letter to Emmy (then his fiancée),
Eberhard writes, "Look only to Jesus! Heb.12:2! He, the crucified and exalted one who gave us our life of faith, will complete

POEMS AND RHYMED PRAYERS

I think upon thy cross, which robs
the devil of his claims on me.

Whate'er befall me, praise or blame,
my old self hangs upon thy Tree,
and thus I'll cry through every land,
"The Lamb of God has died for me!"

And so each day I'm given new faith
to live from him, and him alone.
Yes, he's my vine – my source of life –
for I could not live on my own.

Breslau, October 17, 1905

His blood

O Jesus mine, to thee be honor!
I praise thy spirit's might and fire,
which point me to thy blood, thy cross,
where God creates new life entire.

Praised be the blood that thou hast shed,
which overcomes the power of sin.
Our eyes fixed on the cross, we battle
and watch, though all around looks grim.

To see the cross is to see triumph:
there every evil's done away.

it as well. You will see the same struggle – often rather starkly
expressed – in my poems of 1905. An oppressive awareness of
sin is fully conquered only when one looks to the cross."

So können wir nicht unterliegen,
es schwindet dort der Sünde Wahn.

Ihr starb mein Heiland dort am Kreuze.
Ich darf es glauben, ich starb auch.
O halleluja, ich darf leben
für ihn mit jedes Atems Hauch.

So soll es denn für immer gelten:
Ich lebe nicht mehr selber, nein!
Es lebt in mir mein teurer Jesus.
Ich bleibe Sein im Kreuzesschein.

Breslau, 19. Oktober 1905

Jesus allein

Nichts als Jesum will ich haben,
ihn geniessen Tag für Tag!
Meine Güter, meine Gaben
ich nun nicht mehr sehen mag!

Nichts als Jesum will ich lieben,
ihm nur dienen fort und fort
hier auf Erden wie einst drüben,
wo es sei, an jedem Ort!

Nur an Jesum will ich denken
statt an mich in meiner Not,

In the fall of 1905, Eberhard moved to Halle, where (at his father's insistence, though against his own inclination) he con-

There no one ever is defeated,
by sin's delusion led astray.

My Savior died to conquer sin;
I know, for I too tasted death,
but will henceforth – O hallelujah! –
live for him with every breath.

So let this vow hold true for me:
no longer shall my life be mine,
for thou liv'st in me, dearest Jesus.
Beneath thy cross, I'm always thine.

Breslau, October 19, 1905

Jesus alone

I will have no one but Jesus,
him I'll cherish day by day,
all my gifts, all my possessions
for his love will fling away.

I will love no one but Jesus,
him I'll serve by day and night.
Here on earth, as there in heaven,
every place can show his might.

I will think of none but Jesus,
my own need will now forget,

tinued his studies in theology. As in Breslau, he was soon active
in the local chapter of the German Christian Student Union.

nur in ihn mich stets versenken,
so mich geben in den Tod.

Nur zu Jesu will ich leiten
alle, die mir teuer sind,
ihnen froh den Weg bereiten,
wo ein jeder Gnade find't.

Nur zu Jesu will ich weisen
alle, die mir teuer sind,
dass wir all' den Einen preisen,
in dem jeder Rettung find't.

Nichts als Jesum will ich haben,
fort mit Erdenfreud' und Lust!
Jesus soll mich einzig laben,
tiefes Glück an seiner Brust.

Nichts als Jesum will ich lieben,
brechen ganz mit Weltlichkeit,
alles tun aus heil'gen Trieben,
stets für seinen Ruf bereit!

Halle, 28. Oktober – 1. November 1905

O Jesu, wenn ich dich nur habe,
verblasst mir ganz der Ehre Stern!
Das Kreuz hinfort mich einzig labe,
dort such' ich nichts als meinen Herrn.

Ich freue mich, wenn andre siegen
im grossen Kampf mit Satans Macht,

in him only sink my being,
for his sake is death well met.

I will guide to none but Jesus
all those who to me are dear,
joyfully prepare their pathway
unto him, whose grace is near.

I will lead to none but Jesus
all those whom I love on earth,
that we all may praise together
him who saves us by his birth.

I will have no one but Jesus.
Hence with lust for earth's delights!
Jesus only shall refresh me,
make me happy at his side.

I will love no one but Jesus,
with the world break once for all,
through a holy impulse guided,
always ready for his call.

Halle, October 28–November 1, 1905

O Lord, when you are all I have,
my own star quickly fades from view.
At your cross my thirst is quenched:
I seek for nothing there but you.

When in the fight against the devil
another gains a victory,

wenn Scharen dir zu Füssen liegen,
die sie zu dir ans Kreuz gebracht.

Ich preise dich, wenn viele stehen
im heil'gen Krieg mit deiner Kraft!
O lass sie doch zu allen gehen,
bevor der Tod sie weggerafft!

Ja, Heiland, wen du willst, den sende
zur Rettung armer Seelen aus!
Erwecke dir recht viele Hände,
die Sünder bringen in dein Haus!

Was mich betrifft, so lass mich liegen
an deiner Brust, Johannes gleich!
Mich sehnt nicht mehr nach grossen Siegen,
nein, klein zu sein in deinem Reich!

Im Hintergrunde will ich stehen
und jubeln über andrer Sieg.
Mag alles mir im Staub vergehen,
wenn ich nur dir zu Füssen lieg!

Doch, Herr, willst du mich selber rufen
zum Dienst an deinem Gottesreich,
ich liege vor des Altars Stufen
und folge deinem Wort sogleich.

Dann wirst du selbst mich gründlich beugen,
wie's braucht mein arges, stolzes Herz.
Ich gebe mich dir ganz zu eigen
in heil'ger Freude und im Schmerz.

Halle, 31. Oktober 1905

or when the rescued throngs bow down
before your cross – what joy for me!

I praise you, Lord, for steadfast fighters
who, through your strength, stand in the breach.
O lead them on to countless others
before death sweeps them out of reach!

Yes, Savior, send whoever you will
to bring redemption to poor souls.
Stir many hands to gather in
all sinners into your great halls!

No matter what the future holds,
may I, like John, lie on your breast.
Earth's greatest conquests cannot tempt me;
least in your kingdom, I am blessed.

I'll stand unnoticed happily,
rejoice when other men succeed.
May all I am return to dust,
that I may lie down at your feet.

Yes, Lord, if you choose to call me
to serve your kingdom's coming day,
I'll bow before you at your altar,
hear your word, at once obey.

Then you yourself will shape and mold me
till my haughty heart gives in.
Then will I yield to thee entirely
in happiness, and even in pain.

Halle, October 31, 1905

Die volle Freude hab' ich wieder,
die freie Lust an Jesu Wort.
Sie löst sich frisch in frohe Lieder,
sie preist den Herrn an jedem Ort.

Ich darf für meinen Heiland zeugen
und preisen seine Liebestreu.
Ich will vor ihm mich täglich beugen
und von ihm reden froh und frei.

Der Satan soll mich nicht betrügen,
als sei die Demut immer still.
Der Herr zerstreut die Teufelslügen
und lässt mich zeugen, wenn er will.

Ich schlage meine Hand in seine
und traue fest auf seine Treu.
Und wie gefährlich es auch scheine,
ich folge ihm, wohin es sei!

Halle, 1. November 1905

Nur Jesus, Jesus, andres nicht
ist meines Herzens Kraft und Licht!
Nur Jesus, Jesus, er allein
soll mir für ewig alles sein!

Halle, 1. November 1905

Pure happiness is mine again –
a free delight in Jesus' word
that flows afresh in joyous song.
Where'er I am, I praise the Lord.

I'll witness to my Savior
and to his boundless, faithful love.
I'll bow before the Lord each day
and send my thanks to heaven above.

It is the devil's trick to think
the humble should be always still.
The Lord disperses Satan's lies
and bids me witness at his will.

I'll put my hand in Jesus', then,
and trust his endless loyalty.
However dangerous it seem,
I'll follow him, where'er he be.

Halle, November 1, 1905

O Jesus, Jesus, none but he
shall light my path, and my strength be!
O Jesus, Jesus, he alone –
forever my all and only one.

Halle, November 1, 1905

Jesus, mein König

Brüder! Ich darf Jesum haben,
ihn, den Herren aller Herrn,
darf an seinem Kreuz mich laben.
Ja, sein Auge sieht mich gern!

Ich, Gemeinster der Gemeinen,
darf mich frei dem König nahn,
unrein, wie ich bin dem Reinen,
treten in die Herrscherbahn!

Ja, ich darf den König küssen,
darf an seinem Herzen ruhn.
Jesus möchte keinen missen,
will an allen Gutes tun.

Oh, ich darf beim König bleiben,
bei ihm stehen Tag für Tag.
Jesus wird den Feind vertreiben,
wie er's auch versuchen mag.

Halle, November 1905

Ans Kreuz

Den Blick nur fest aufs Kreuz gerichtet,
von aller Schmach und Sünde fort!
So wird das Dunkel gleich gelichtet,
der Schatten muss verschwinden dort!

Mit ganzer Kraft hinweggewendet
von jedem Zug des eignen Ich,

Jesus, my king

Brothers, Christ has let me take
him to my heart – the Lord of lords –
has welcomed me, my thirst to slake;
my tired soul at his cross restores.

I, though meaner than the meanest,
may still come before his throne;
though impure before his pureness
in his footsteps still may go.

Yes, the King accepts my kisses,
lets me rest against his heart.
He turns from no one, no one misses,
but to *all* his good imparts.

Yes, he bids me stay beside him,
lets me stand by him each day,
and though the Foe's attacks be grim,
Jesus drives them all away.

Halle, November 1905

To the cross

When on the cross I fix my gaze,
freed from the curse of sin and shame,
then dark will yield, and light's bright rays
drive back the shadows whence they came.

With all my strength, I will defy
the ego's baseness and its guile.

das immer wieder Jesum schändet,
so oft es sagt: Denk auch an dich!

Verhasst sei mir mein eignes Wesen
mit seinem Stolz und böser Lust.
Ich werde niemals je genesen
als – tot in mir – an Jesu Brust!

So nimm mich denn, mein teurer König!
Dein Sterben ist für mich genug.
Und fühle ich auch noch so wenig,
ich höre nicht auf Satans Trug.

Du siegst! Du hast mich überwunden,
am Kreuze nahmst du mich mit dir!
In schweren wie in frohen Stunden
bleib' ich gestorben dort wie hier!

Halle, November 1905

Herr Jesu, nimm mein eignes Leben,
ich hasse mich von Herzensgrund.
Dir will ich mich für immer geben,
mich weihen dir in heil'gem Bund.

Ich glaube, Herr, du kannst die Schlechten
und ganz Gesunknen machen rein.
Du kannst sie einzig zu Gerechten
so wandeln, dass sie werden dein!

Du kannst auch mich gemeinen Sünder
durch deine Gnade machen frei.

"Think of yourself!" – its artful cry
strikes Jesus' face, seeks to defile.

My inborn nature – lust and pride
and all their evils – I detest.
I'll not be whole until I lie,
dead to myself, on Jesus' breast.

Accept me, then, my Lord and my King:
your death for me will yet suffice.
Though I know naught of suffering,
I'll not give ear to Satan's lies.

You conquer, and I'm overpowered!
To your own cross you take me too.
In joyful as in trying hours,
there, dead to self, I live for you.

Halle, November 1905

Lord Jesus, take my very life.
I loathe myself right to the core,
and so I give myself to you –
a holy bond forevermore.

I know that you can take, O Lord,
the vilest man and cleanse his soul.
Yes, by your power you can transform him,
make him righteous, pure, and whole.

Yes, even a sinner as mean as I
can be made free by your great grace,

Nimm mich ins Reich der Gotteskinder;
in deiner Kraft ich bleibe treu!

O Jesu, König, sei gepriesen
für deine Bluts- und Feuerkraft!
Ans Kreuz, ans Kreuz hast du gewiesen,
das neue, reine Menschen schafft!

Halle, November 1905

Herr, beuge mich in tiefe Tiefen,
wirf mich vor dir in heil'gen Staub!
Wie viele auch von Gnade riefen,
ich sehe mich, der Sünden Raub!

Ich bin der Schlechteste von allen,
und meine Schuld schreit auf zu dir!
Hast du an mir denn noch Gefallen,
der ich ein Abscheu bin selbst mir?

Wie lange hast du mich getragen,
die Schlange, treu an deiner Brust?
Ich durft' es immer wieder wagen,
in dir zu suchen meine Lust.

Und ich, ich habe dir gelohnet
mit ruchlosem Verrat die Treu';
ich hab' dein Herze nicht geschonet.
Wie spät kam immer erst die Reu'!

Was nützte sie, wenn sie nicht endet
der Sünde fürchterliche Macht?

so take me into your children's realm,
there to dwell in strength and faith.

All honor and praise be yours, my king,
for your blood's power, your fire pure!
And praise the cross you point us to,
where man, new made, is true and sure!

Halle, November 1905

Lord, bring me to my knees in dust,
bow low my head, and hear my prayer!
Though others sing of your great grace,
I still fall into every snare.

Of all men, I'm by far the worst –
it cries to heaven above, my guilt.
How can you still have hope for me,
who, seeing myself, with loathing fill?

And yet how long you've carried me,
a serpent, on your loving breast –
you've given me courage ever anew,
my heart's desire, and my mind's rest.

But I returned your patient love
with base betrayal; never lent
a hand to guard you, care for you –
put off remorse, would not repent.

I doubted in the purpose
of fighting sin unceasingly.

Was war sie wert, wenn wieder schändet
mein Herz die Kraft, die du gebracht?

Doch nein, auch ich verfluchter Sünder
soll zu dir kommen, wie ich bin –
zu dir, dem starken Überwinder,
der selbst den Teufel raffte hin.

Ich glaube jetzt, ich kann vertrauen,
du siegst auch über mich am Kreuz!
Ich will auf deine Gnade bauen
und widerstehen jedem Reiz.

So will ich glauben! Es mag kosten
soviel es will, ich bleibe dein!
Am Kreuze weiss ich alle Lasten
und bin von aller Sünde rein.

Halle, November 1905

Jesus am Kreuz

Siehst du Jesum bleich am Kreuze,
wie er dort hängt in Todesqual?
Trieb ihn nicht auch deine Sünde
zu dieser furchtbar schweren Wahl?

Sieh den König aller Welten
im Machtbereich der Satanswut!
Todeshauch legt Eiseskälte
um ihn, der nichts dawider tut!

I thought: why bother, when with each step,
I squander what you offer me?

But no! Even I, accurséd wretch,
must come just as I am to you
whose love disarms and conquers all,
the devil himself o'erpowers too.

For I believe that I, too, can
be helped and rescued by your cross.
I'll build henceforth on grace, and spurn
all sin's desire in me, all dross.

I will believe! Cost what it may,
I'm yours, for by your sacrifice
upon the cross my heart's been cleansed,
found rest and peace beyond all price.

Halle, November 1905

Christ on the cross

Don't you see the Savior hanging
deathly pale upon the cross?
Was it not your sin that drove him
to this harsh and dreadful choice?

See him, king of all creation,
held fast by Satan's angry grip,
surrounded by death's ice-cold air –
yet he does nothing to resist.

Weisst du, dass er Todesschmerzen
für dich aus Liebeswillen trug,
dass er gedacht an unsre Herzen,
als man ihm blut'ge Wunden schlug?

Hast du wirklich eingesehen
und hat es dich ans Herz gefasst,
dass diese Qualen nur geschehen,
damit du endlich Frieden hast?

Dann ist sicher dein Verlangen,
dass dieser Tod dir Leben wird,
dass für immer alles Bangen
beendigt unser treuer Hirt!

Oh, wir wollen seinen Qualen
reifen lassen reine Frucht.
Was an uns nicht kann gefallen,
muss hinweg mit aller Wucht!

Ist das ganze alte Wesen
wirklich an dem Kreuze tot,
können wir erst ganz genesen,
sind wir frei von aller Not.

Dann ist Jesu Ziel erworben,
eher ist es nicht erreicht.
Dazu ist der Herr gestorben,
für uns in Todesqual erbleicht.

Halle, November 1905

Don't you know the agonies
of death he bore for love of you?
That for your soul he endured it,
to be wounded, bloodied so?

Have you truly comprehended –
has it struck your inmost heart,
that he suffered all this anguish
so that peace might be your part?

Surely it must be your longing
that his death mean life for you,
and that all your fears be ended,
vanquished by your shepherd true.

Let his bitter torment, then,
work in you and bring forth pure fruit.
Whatever causes him displeasure
grasp at once, weed out, uproot.

Once your old and evil works,
laid at the cross, are truly dead,
then you will be fully healed,
free from worry, pain, and dread.

Then Christ's goal will be achieved –
but only then, and not before,
which is why he bore such sorrow,
had to die in anguish sore.

Halle, November 1905

Rette Seelen!

Herr, wir bringen dir die Seelen,
die heute lauschen auf dein Wort.
Dir wollen wir sie still befehlen,
du wirkst auf sie an jedem Ort.

Jesu, lass sie nie vergessen,
dass du für sie gestorben bist!
Lass sie es ernst vor dir ermessen,
vertreib den Feind mit seiner List!

Bringe heute sie zum Frieden,
stell ihnen deine Gnade dar,
dass sie einst droben wie hienieden
gehören zu der Deinen Schar!

Halle, November 1905

Rette, rette, Herr, Verlorne,
die fern von dir in Sünde sind!
Sind wir doch alle Staubgeborne,
bei dir doch jeder Rettung find't.

Fluch und Schande trennen Seelen
zu Hunderten von Gott dem Herrn!
Oh, du wirst dir Männer wählen,
die sich dir opfern froh und gern.

Rescue them!

Lord, the souls we bring to thee
today will listen to thy word.
We commend them to thee humbly.
Change their hearts, let them be stirred.

Jesus, let them ne'er forget
how, on the cross, for them you died.
May they contemplate this truth
and drive out Satan with his lies.

Bring thy peace to them this day
and set thy grace before them too,
so that they might, here and in heaven,
be counted in thy multitude.

Halle, November 1905

Rescue, Lord, the lost of earth,
those trapped in sin, those far from you.
Though born of dust – as are we all –
through you they'll find redemption too.

Bitter shame still separates
so many souls from your kind eyes,
but you need men prepared for battle,
glad to sacrifice their lives.

Hab Erbarmen mit den Sündern!
Lass Zeugen reden von dem Heil!
Mache sie zu Gotteskindern!
An deinem Reich gib ihnen Teil!

Halle, November 1905

Jesus im Schiff

Warum wollt ihr noch Sorge hegen?
Der Heiland ist ja selbst im Schiff!
Bei Jesus kann kein Sturm sich regen,
der seine Jünger wirft ans Riff.

Warum wollt ihr nicht Glauben fassen?
Er steht ja selber vorn am Bug!
In keiner Not wird er uns lassen,
die Furcht ist nichts als Satans Trug.

Drum weg mit allem schwachen Zittern,
denn Christus ist ja selbst im Kahn!
Bei Stille wie in Ungewittern
führt Jesus uns auf sicherer Bahn!

Halle, November 1905

Before moving to Halle in the fall of 1905, Eberhard spent a vacation on the North Sea island of Langeoog. He later wrote that seeing the sea whipped into high waves by storm winds,

Have mercy, then, on all who sin.
Let witnesses your grace declare.
Save them, turn them into children –
in your kingdom let them share.

Halle, November 1905

Christ in the ship

Be not afraid, for naught will hurt you,
the Lord himself is in the ship!
Where Jesus is, no storm can harm you,
no wind can throw you on the cliff.

Hold on in faith, he will be with you.
He stands in front, right in the bow!
In all your need he'll not forsake you.
Leave Satan's fear behind you now.

Away with all your fearful trembling,
for in your boat is Christ himself!
In stillness and in stormy weather
he leads us safe past rocky shelf.

Halle, November 1905

and then turning calm – all in obedience to the forces of nature – helped him submit to his father's wishes (i.e. to continue
studying theology) and to trust in God's leading.

Aus dem Tode, Leben

Der Sünde ganz gestorben
und lebend nur für Ihn!
Den Sieg hat er erworben,
vor dem wir sinken hin!

Ich will es fröhlich glauben,
dass alles abgetan.
Kein Feind soll mir es rauben,
der Herr tilgt jeden Bann!

Ich will mich drauf verlassen,
dass Jesu Wort nicht lügt.
Ich kann mein Leben hassen,
das mich so oft betrügt.

Ich kann mich Gott ergeben,
dass er nur lebt in mir,
dass ihm gehört mein Leben,
ich ihm schon atme hier.

Ich darf auf Jesum trauen,
dass ich durch seine Kraft
auf nichts mehr werde bauen,
als das, was er mir schafft.

Ich glaube fest er sieget!
Sein Grab ist aufgetan.
Ja, Satan unterlieget.
Der Herr ist auf dem Plan!

Halle, Dezember 1905

Out of death, life

Completely dead to sin,
I live for Christ. The crown
of victory is his.
To him I must bow down.

With joy I will believe it:
his power has conquered all.
Of this no foe may rob me,
for God breaks every thrall.

I know without a doubt
that Christ's word never lies.
It is *my* life I ought to hate,
for its deceitful guise.

I'll give myself to God –
for no other will I strive.
Each breath I draw is his,
who alone keeps me alive.

I'll put my hope in Jesus,
for apart from his own power
there's nothing else to build on,
but what he gives each hour.

I firmly trust he'll triumph.
His grave is empty, bare.
The devil is defeated:
Christ conquers everywhere!

Halle, December 1905

Frei durchs Kreuz

O Jesu, deine Schmerzen,
du littest sie für mich,
damit an deinem Herzen
genesen kann auch ich.

Du willst aus allen Nöten
befrein mein armes Herz.
Du willst das alles töten,
das mir bereitet Schmerz.

Ja, alle meine Sorgen,
sie gehen auf in dir!
Du willst an jedem Morgen
den Frieden geben mir!

Du hast für mich erworben
am Kreuz ein volles Heil.
Du bist für mich gestorben!
Ich hab am Leben teil!

Halle, Dezember 1905

Ich glaube für Seelen,
ich lasse sie nie.
Ich will es erwählen
zu leben für sie.

On June 2, 1907, Eberhard wrote to Emmy, "I believe I shall never regret having worked with souls for Jesus, and I must

Freed by the cross

Your bitter pains, dear Jesus –
you suffered them for me –
that, on your heart now resting,
I might be healed and freed.

You seek to free my heart
from misery each day;
whatever grieves and pains me
you stamp out and take away.

From all my care and burdens
I find relief in you;
on each and every morning
you give me peace anew.

You bought me full salvation
upon the cross. 'Twas there
you suffered death for my sake,
and now your life I share.

Halle, December 1905

With faith for each soul,
I trust and believe.
I've chosen to live for them,
never to leave.

hold to the fact that it was the Spirit that urged me to it, even
though much of it was weak and wrong."

Ich liebe die Brüder,
ich lasse sie nicht.
Ich will immer wieder
sie suchen im Licht.

Halle, ca. 1905

Mein Gott, bewahre mir den Segen,
erhalt in mir den Geist der Kraft!
Lass sich kein fremdes Feuer regen,
nur das, was Jesus selber schafft.

O Gott, erhalte mir den Glauben,
der freudig stützt sich auf dein Wort,
lass mir ihn nie durch Menschen rauben,
ja, gib mir Sieg an jedem Ort!

Mein Jesus, halt mich in der Liebe
zu Gott, dem Vater, und zu dir,
dass mit des Geistes reinem Triebe
ich stündlich bete: Bleib bei mir!

Lass fest mich in der Hoffnung stehen,
dass du bald kommst in Herrlichkeit!
Dann will ich dir entgegengehen
und bei dir sein in Ewigkeit!

Halle, Semesteranfang, April 1906

At the start of the summer semester, 1906, Eberhard moved into the Silesian Seminary of the Lutheran Church. He was elected chairman of the Halle chapter of the German Christian

I love all my brothers –
for them will I fight,
steadfastly seeking
each one in the light.

Halle, ca. 1905

Lord, let thy blessing rest on me.
Give me the pow'r of thy spirit's flame,
for I would fan no other fire
but that which burns in Jesus' name.

O God, protect in me the faith
that rests in joy upon thy word.
Let no one shatter my belief:
grant victories throughout the world.

Uphold me, Jesus, in my love
to God the Father and to thee,
that with the Spirit's pure desire
I might pray hourly: stay with me!

O let me live in hope that thou
wilt soon return in majesty.
How gladly then I'll go to meet thee,
be with thee eternally.

Halle, at the start of the semester, April 1906

Student Union around the same time. In his inaugural address
he said, "Only Jesus! That is the motto of our movement."

O Herr, du weisst, worum ich bitte:
dass du mich lenkst mit sanftem Geist.
O leite sicher meine Tritte,
da du allein den Richtweg weisst!

Ja, Jesu, komm mit deinem Segen
und nagle mich ganz fest ans Kreuz.
Lass nur mein Ich sich nicht mehr regen,
halt ganz mich frei von eitlem Reiz.

Mein Heiland, deine Kraft ist stärker
als alle, alle Menschenmacht!
Du brachtest mich aus finsterm Kerker
dahin wo hell die Sonne lacht.

Du kannst mich nun auch weiter führen,
dass nie von dir ich weiche ab.
Du lässt mich deine Treue spüren,
du leitest mich mit sicherm Stab.

Mein Hirte, du kannst mich nicht lassen,
in dir bin ich geborgen fest.
Lass freudig deine Hand mich fassen,
die keinen je verirren lässt!

Halle, 15. August 1906

O Lord, you know my heart's request:
that you might lead and gently guide,
for you must show which way is best.
O steer my feet; stay at my side.

Yes, Jesus, come, give me your blessing.
Nail me firmly to your cross,
and when I rear my proud, vain head,
purge me of all foolishness.

From dungeon dark you led me upward
into the sunshine's bright, clear light.
O Savior mine, your strength o'erpowers
all human strength, all human might.

Now, as I journey onward, lead me
and never let me turn from you.
Your faithfulness is always there.
Your staff will guide me safely through.

My shepherd, you will always hold me.
You are my refuge, safe and true.
With joy I feel your arms enfold me:
you'll never let me stray from you.

Halle, August 15, 1906

Jesus will dich gänzlich haben,
ohne Schranken ganz für sich:
deine Liebe, deine Gaben –
opfre ihm in Wahrheit dich!

Blut'ger Ernst ist hier vonnöten,
völlig ganz ergebner Sinn!
Furchtbar ist's, sein Ich zu töten
und sein Herzblut geben hin.

Aber, Herr, für dich ist alles,
Leib und Leben, alles dein!
Willst du's, Liebster, gut, so fall' es;
nichts will ich mehr nennen mein.

Kost' es mir auch Glück und Freude,
du bist's, den ich haben will.
Du bleibst mir im tiefsten Leide,
machst mein Herze fest und still.

Du, mein Jesus, bleibst mein Leben,
alles andre opfre ich.
Nichts als dich will ich erstreben,
dich, mein Heiland, einzig dich!

Halle, 16. August 1906

Jesus longs to make you his –
entirely, utterly his own.
So bring him all your love and gifts,
and lay your self before his throne.

It takes a fierce resolve to yield –
to give yourself, and never swerve.
It takes the death of selfishness
and your life's blood to truly serve.

Yet I would give these gladly, Lord.
Take life and limb: they are yours.
Whate'er you wish – so be it.
All I have is mine no more.

And though it cost me happiness,
you remain my heart's true balm,
for you are near me, even in grief,
you give me courage, peace, and calm.

I'll sacrifice my all for you –
dear Jesus, you are all I own.
I have no other goal in life
but you, my Savior – you alone.

Halle, August 16, 1906

O Jesu, Heiland, viel zu wenig
liebt dich doch meine Seele noch.
Leg mir, mein Meister, Herr und König,
viel fester auf dein sanftes Joch!

Entzünd in mir das heil'ge Feuer,
das ewig brennt, ohn' Unterlass;
denn keine Sache ist zu teuer:
Gib Liebe mir ohn' Grenz und Mass.

Lass eine Glut in mir entbrennen,
die nichts auf Erden löschen kann!
Lass dich allein mich Herren nennen,
dein eigen sein als ganzer Mann!

Ja, Jesu, so mich dir zu geben
ist grösste Freude mir und Lust!
O nimm, o nimm mein ganzes Leben,
dein Feuer glüh' in meiner Brust.

Halle, 17. August 1906

Eberhard prayed, as the last line of this poem says, for God's
fire to "burn in my breast," and according to those who knew
him, it did – so much so that he was soon regarded (along with

I still lack love, O Jesus mine –
too little is my love for thee.
So place more firmly, Lord and King,
I beg, thy gentle yoke on me.

Kindle in me the holy flame
that burns forever and will not cease.
No price can be too high, so long
as thy love in me doth increase.

So let your flame consume me, that
no pow'r on earth can quench its glow.
Yes, none but thee shall I call Master.
A man complete, I am thine own.

Yes, Lord, I give myself to thee
in greatest joy and happiness.
O take, I pray, my life entire,
and let thy fire burn in my breast.

Halle, August 17, 1906

the evangelist Ludwig von Gerdtell, his mentor) as "the" voice
of the revival movement then sweeping Halle.

Ströme des Segens vom Herrn wir flehten,
Ströme des Segens auf lechzendes Land.
Sehnend wir traten mit sieghaftem Beten
freudig vor den, der einst starb und erstand.

Kamen sie auch nicht mit mächtigem Rauschen,
sondern verborgen für den, der nicht sieht,
leise wir hörten mit freudigem Lauschen,
immer vernehmlicher, jubelndes Lied!

Jubel wir hörten für volle Erlösung,
Jubel für gnädig erfahrenes Heil!
Jubel für längst schon ersehnte Genesung,
Ströme der Freude uns wurden zuteil!

Endlich es wagten nun zagende Brüder,
blindlings zu trauen auf Gott und sein Wort.
Dankend, nun nahmen wir wieder und wieder
Zuflucht zu Jesu, dem Retter und Hort.

Endlich jetzt wurden wir fest und entschieden,
endlich bereit zum Gehorsam der Tat,
siegreich dem Feind ein Halt! zu gebieten:
Häufig genug er betrogen uns hat!

Ströme des Segens hat Gott uns gegeben!
Ströme des Segens für jeden, der will,
Ströme auf unser erschlaffendes Leben!
Ströme des Segens, beständig und still!

Halle, Semesterschluss, September 1906

Remembering the Halle revival movement, and this poem in
particular, Emmy writes in her memoirs that "we were filled
with a deep love to Christ and used each free minute to grow
deeper, to learn songs of an inner nature, and to testify to

Begging the Lord to show'r us with blessings,
to let down his rain on the parched land below,
we came before him with confident prayers,
trusting in One who died and arose.

And blessings came, though not with the storm wind,
and hidden from those whose eyes cannot see;
and as we eagerly listened, we heard it:
a joyous song rising, glad and free.

Jubilant joy in redemption complete!
Joy in salvation and knowledge of grace!
Joy in recovery, long awaited!
Streams of joy on each uplifted face!

Brothers who'd wavered now finally dared,
though blind, to trust in God and his Word.
Grateful, again and again we took refuge
in Jesus Christ, our Savior and guard.

Finally, firm and decisive and ready
at last to obey God's call with deeds,
we cried out, victoriously, "Halt!" to the devil –
we'd fallen too often for his deceit.

Yes, God has sent us a shower of blessings.
To any who begs, he'll gladly send –
streams to refresh us when we are weary,
rivers that quietly flow without end.

Halle, at the end of the semester, September 1906

Christ. All of us felt an urgency to carry the message to others,
to bear witness to Christ. Our prayer meetings were a great
source of strength. This song expresses…the spirit that swept
through the country like a wind at that time."

EBERHARD ARNOLD

Sieg!

Lass nur Satan weiter toben
mit Gewalt und feiger List.
Ich will laut den Herren loben,
den Erretter Jesum Christ.

Will er listig mich verführen
nachzugeben eitlem Stolz,
will er meinen Hochmut schüren,
blick' ich auf das Marterholz.

Dort, wo Jesus hat gelitten,
sank mein Ich in Todesnacht.
Er hat mir den Sieg erstritten,
er zerbrach des Teufels Macht!

Halle, 1906

Jesus

Lange hast du mich gerufen,
dass ich lebte ganz für dich,
dass ich auf des Altars Stufen
endlich opferte mein Ich!

Doch wie lang ich widerstanden,
heute stell' ich mich dir dar.

As his involvement with the revival movement grew,
Eberhard's gifts as a leader were affirmed, and he was invited to
lead bible studies, chair conferences, and hold public addresses
in other cities. Along with such distinctions (he was "only" a

Victory!

Satan's cunning never ceases –
let the violent coward rage.
I will raise my voice in song,
my redeemer, Christ, to praise.

If he tricks me or misleads me
to give in to sinful pride,
or tries to feed my vanity,
to the cross I'll turn my eyes.

For there, where Jesus bore such pain,
I drowned my ego in death's night.
'Tis there he conquered all for me,
there that he broke Satan's might.

Halle, 1906

Jesus

How long hast thou been calling me
to give my life entire to thee,
to sacrifice my ego
before thy altar finally!

And I have long resisted. But today
I plead: Lord, loose my bonds.

student) came the temptation of pride, but also the honesty to
acknowledge, fight, and ultimately reject it – which he did, as
these poems make clear.

Löse mich von allen Banden!
Ich ergeb' mich ganz und gar.

Gänzlich will ich jetzt entsagen
aller Weichlichkeit und Lust.
Freudig will ich's heute wagen,
dir zu fallen an die Brust.

Alles feige, schlaffe Bangen
geb' ich siegreich in den Tod!
Ja, ich darf dahin gelangen,
dass ich lebe nur für Gott.

Keine Stunde, keine Gabe,
nichts mehr ist nun da für mich.
Was ich bin und was ich habe
bin ich, Gott, allein für dich!

Lange hat der Feind gerungen,
uns zu rauben unsern Sieg.
Doch der Herr hat ihn bezwungen,
als er einst das Kreuz bestieg.

Und wir durften es erleben,
dass des Kreuzes Siegeskraft
aus dem alten, feigen Beben
starkes, neues Leben schafft.

Ja, wir wollen froh vertrauen,
dass der Sieg ein ew'ger ist,
wollen fest auf Jesum schauen,
unsern Retter, unsern Christ!

Halle, 1906

For I would come before thy face
and give myself into thy hands.

From this day on I will renounce
all selfish flabbiness, all lust;
with joy and gratefulness will dare
to cast myself upon thy breast.

All slackness, cowardice, and fear
I now reject and put to death.
From this moment, I must live
for God alone with every breath.

Every hour and every gift –
all that I am and all I own –
no longer can I count them mine,
for they belong to God alone.

And though the Enemy's fought long
to wrest this victory from me,
I know the cross has laid him low,
has robbed death's sting eternally.

For I have seen, without a doubt,
what on the cross the Lord can do:
he takes the trembling coward, gives him
strength and vigor, life anew.

Yes, I will trust, rejoicing
that his victories endure fore'er,
and firmly fix my eyes on him:
on Jesus Christ, my Savior sure.

Halle, 1906

Gib mir ein Herz, o lieber Vater,
das, ganz vom eignen Willen frei,
nur dir gehorcht, dem Berater,
und dein Gebot erfüllet treu!

Gib mir ein Herz, das gerne übet
die Selbstverleugnung jederzeit,
das alle seine Feinde liebet,
gewiss der letzten Herrlichkeit.

Gib mir ein Herz, das stets Erbarmen
mit tiefgesunknen Menschen hat,
und sie umfängt mit Liebesarmen
und führt zur schönen Vaterstadt.

Gib mir ein Herz, das gänzlich ferne
von Eigennutz und Weltlust ist,
den Armen, Durst'gen hilft so gerne
und ganz sich selbst dabei vergisst.

Gib mir ein Herz, das niemals achtet
Verfolgung, Ängste, Hohn und Spott;
wenn man es auch beschimpft, verachtet,
stets Treue hält zu seinem Gott!

Ein solches Herz, das muss ich haben,
wie deines ist, so gottgesinnt.
Nimm, Jesu, mich und alle Gaben!
In dir allein dies Herz ich find'!

Halle, 1906

Give me a heart, dear heavenly Father,
a heart that's free of all self-will,
a heart obedient to thy counsel,
that gladly thy commands fulfills.

Give me a heart prepared to practice
true self-denial at any time,
a heart that loves its enemies,
assured of glories yet to come.

Give me a heart of sympathy
for every person mired in sin,
that guides them toward the Father's land,
embraces them, and takes them in.

Give me a heart that hankers not
for worldly pleasures, selfish ends,
a heart that loves the poor, and so
forgets itself, a hand to lend.

Give me a heart that pays no heed
to threats or scorn or ridicule,
that keeps faith always with its God,
though blamed, despised, or called a fool.

A heart like thine, that lives for God –
would such a heart be given to me!
O Jesus, take me and all my gifts:
I'll find this heart alone in thee.

Halle, 1906

Gib mir den Geist, mein treuer Vater,
den Geist, der durch die Seele geht,
den Geist als einzigen Berater,
der treibt zu dir mich ins Gebet.

Gib mir den Geist der gar nichts duldet
von eignem Wesen, Mut und Stolz,
der zeigt, wie tief ich mich verschuldet,
wie nichts an mir als dürres Holz.

Gib mir den Geist, der tief mich beuget
vor deinem heil'gen Angesicht,
auf Jesum, den Erlöser zeiget,
der jedem bringt Heil und Gericht.

Gib mir den Geist, der alles fliehet,
was Anerkennung ist und Ruhm,
der jeden Sinn zu Jesus ziehet
und beugend ehrt sein Königtum.

Gib mir den Geist, der brünstig ringet
um Seelen, die in finsterm Tod,
der dir sie alle, alle bringet,
dass du sie rettest aus der Not!

Gib mir den Geist, der einzig streitet
um deine Ehre, heil'ger Gott,
der deine Herrschaft ausgebreitet,
seitdem dein Sohn besiegt den Tod!

Halle, 1906

Father, grant to me the spirit
that penetrates my very soul
and drives it, as its surest guide,
in prayer to thee, my only goal.

Grant me the spirit that rejects
self-will, self-confidence, and pride.
Show me my deep guilt, for I
am naught but dead wood – withered, dry.

Grant me the spirit, Lord, that moves me
to kneel before thy holy face,
that points to my redeemer, Christ,
who judges all, but gives all grace.

Grant me the spirit that recoils
from recognition and renown,
that draws my every thought to Christ,
and bows in reverence at his throne.

Grant me the spirit, Lord, of fervor
that wrests the lost from death's dark night,
that rescues every one from pain
and brings them into thy pure light.

Grant me the spirit that endeavors
to praise thee alone with every breath,
and spreads forevermore thy realm,
and thy Son's triumph over death.

Halle, 1906

Bis auf den Grund! (Matth. 5, 3–10)

Bis auf den Grund mach arm uns, Jesu!
Mach uns vom Reichtum gänzlich bloss,
dass wir in dir nur haben Leben.
Ja, löse uns von allem los!

Bis auf den Grund mach ernst uns, Jesu,
vertiefe uns in Schmerz und Leid,
dass wir die schwere Not der Welten
empfinden tief und allezeit!

Bis auf den Grund mach gut uns, Jesu,
bis auf den Grund dir wesensgleich,
wie du es bist in deinem Leiden:
im Tode noch an Liebe reich!

Bis auf den Grund gib Durst uns, Jesu!
Wecke den Hunger, nie gestillt!
Mach immer tiefer das Verlangen,
das stets zu einem ist gewillt.

Bis auf den Grund gib uns Erbarmen,
bis auf den Grund Barmherzigkeit!
Dass Liebe gibt sich hin den Armen,
in Güte mach die Seele weit!

Bis auf den Grund mach rein uns, Jesu,
du, dessen Herz so völlig rein!
Gib uns dich selbst, dein reines Wesen,
und mach uns einzig, gänzlich dein!

First published in a Baptist newspaper in September 1915, this
poem was revised more than once by Eberhard. Though the first

Completely thine! (Matt. 5:3–10)

Make us completely poor, O Jesus,
from wealth and riches set us free.
Yes, strip us bare of all our things,
that we have life alone in thee.

Make us completely earnest, Jesus,
and deepen us through pain and woe,
that we may feel the heavy weight
of the world's pain, where'er we go.

Make us completely good, O Jesus,
according to God's image above,
and good like thee, who, suffering
and dying, was yet filled with love.

Make us completely thirsty, Jesus.
Give us a hunger none can still.
Make thou our longing greater yet,
at all times but to will one will.

Let thy compassion and thy mercy
rule us entirely, all our days.
That we in love may serve the poor,
widen our hearts and souls through grace.

Make us completely clean, O Jesus,
thou, whose own heart is fully pure.
Make us entirely thine, we plead:
give us thyself, thy nature sure.

version was written in the first-person singular "me" throughout, he later introduced the plural "us."

Bis auf den Grund mach fest uns, Jesu,
bis auf den Grund im Sterben fest.
Mach stark das Herz, in dir zu dulden,
dass niemals Herz von Herze lässt.

Bis auf den Grund lass mich durchdringen
den Glauben an dein reines Blut!
Lass alle Saiten mir erklingen
in diesem tiefsten Glaubensgut.

Halle, ca. 1906

Aus tiefster Seel' gib mir Verlangen,
aus tiefster Seel' den heissen Durst,
dass alles in mir sich sehnt nach Segen,
den du im Glauben geben wirst.

Aus tiefster Seele lass mich beten
im Glauben an dein Wort und Blut;
gewiss und sicher lass mich treten
vor dich, als den, der Wunder tut.

Aus tiefster Seele lass mich loben,
aus tiefster Seele jubeln frei,
dass du, mein Herr und König droben
mich gnädig segnest täglich neu!

Halle, ca. 1906

These three verses were included in an early version of the
previous poem.

Make us completely firm, O Jesus,
though pain and death tear us apart.
Give us thy strength, that we endure,
that nothing can divide our hearts.

Completely penetrate and fill me
with trust in thy pure blood, O Lord,
and let each string within me sound
faith's deepest good in one great chord.

Halle, ca. 1906

From my soul's depths, I beg you, Lord:
give me the burning thirst that yearns
for nothing but the grace you give
to him who, trusting, toward you turns.

From my soul's depths, O let my prayer
with faith in your word and blood arise!
Lord, you who work great miracles:
let me stand firm before your eyes.

From my soul's depths, let me rejoice
and freely sing my praise to you –
yes, from its depths, to my king above,
who blesses me daily with grace anew.

Halle, ca. 1906

Herr, du bist der treue Hirte
der den Seinen hilft im Streit.
Ja, du willst mir helfen weiter,
dass ich siege stets wie heut.

Nimm die Hand des schwachen Jüngers,
halt sie fest in deiner, Herr!
Lenk die Schritte! Leit die Tritte,
dass ich wanke nimmermehr!

Gib die Festigkeit des Geistes,
die du einem Petrus gabst!
Gib sie mir, dem schwachen Streiter,
der nur siegt, wenn du ihn labst.

Lass den Geist herniederkommen,
rauschend, strömend jetzt auf mich!
Ist die Flamme fast verglommen,
mach sie lodern mächtiglich!

Du allein kannst Feuer geben,
Feuer leuchtend, rein und heiss!
Nur in dir ist alles Leben,
dir allein drum Ruhm und Preis!

Halle, ca. 1906

Lord and faithful shepherd, thou
who guid'st thy flock through every fray,
I know thou wilt always help me
conquer, as I did today.

Guide me, Lord, a weak disciple.
Take my hand, and hold it fast.
Lead me, that I may not stumble
but walk firmly in thy path.

Grant me, Lord, as thou didst Peter,
a spirit steady, firm and clear,
for I am but a weak fighter,
winning only when thou'rt near.

Let thy spirit down from heaven,
roaring, rushing over me!
When my flame begins to die,
rekindle it more powerfully.

Only thou canst set my heart
on fire and make it truly blaze.
Thou alone art life and breath:
to thee alone be thanks and praise.

Halle, ca. 1906

Es war ein Jahr der reichen Gnade,
das du mir, Herr, aus Liebe gabst.
Du führest mich auf lichte Pfade,
mit tiefer Freude du mich labst!

O nimm, o nimm mein ganzes Leben
dir jetzt als volles Opfer hin!
Ich geb' es dir ohn' Widerstreben,
erfülle du mir Herz und Sinn!

O Herr, du hast mich ganz erworben.
Nichts Halbes darf an mir mehr sein!
Du bist für mich den Tod gestorben,
nun bin ich ewig, einzig dein!

So lass im neuen Jahr mich leben
an deiner Hand, für dich allein!
Bewahre mich vor falschem Streben!
Ich will dir dienen völlig rein.

Nur du kannst mich mit Kraft erfüllen
zur Arbeit in des Tages Müh'.
Nur du kannst all mein Sehnen stillen,
mir Frieden geben spät und früh.

In deiner Kraft will ich bestehen
den heil'gen Kampf auch dieses Jahr,
stets vorwärts, niemals rückwärts gehen
und dir gehorchen ganz und gar!

Halle oder Breslau, Neujahr 1907

This year was one of richest grace,
that thou in love didst give to me.
On paths of light hast thou me led,
with deep joy filled me, set me free.

Accept me, Lord, take my whole life:
I give it thee in every part
without resistance or reserve.
Fill thou alone my mind and heart.

Lord, I was dearly bought by thee:
may no half-heartedness be mine.
Death's agony didst thou endure.
Now and eternally I'm thine.

O may I live, in this new year,
for thee alone, led by thy hand.
Save me from errant striving, Lord.
To serve thee purely, here I stand.

Thou only giv'st, to bear the strain
of daily toil, the strength I need.
Thou still'st the yearnings of my heart.
To live in thee is peace indeed.

Alone in thy strength can I face
the holy fight within the year,
and forward, never backward, look,
obey thy voice, and thy word hear.

Halle or Breslau, January 1, 1907

An Emmy

Es war im Mondenschein
dort draussen in der Heide,
da wandert' ich allein.

Des Waldes Finsternis
durchbrachen Silberstreifen
in wildem Schattenriss.

Weithin war alles stumm,
es krächzte nur die Eule,
sonst Schweigen ringsherum.

In mir ging Grosses vor.
In dieser Nacht der Nächte
mein Herze ich verlor.

Ich dachte nur an sie.
O dass sie bei mir wäre,
mich nie verliesse, nie!

Mich dünkt, sie wär' bei mir,
als hört' ich ihre Schritte
und schaut' ins Auge ihr.

Welch grosses, tiefes Glück,
ihr Angesicht zu sehen!
O wich' es nie zurück!

On March 26, 1907, after an evening Bible study, Eberhard took Emmy to her home, and they had their first "real talk" (they had met before but not exchanged more than a few words). Later Eberhard wrote to her, "After leaving you…in the moonlight, I prayed long and earnestly on my knees and received the certainty that you would become mine. I then went

To Emmy

Beneath a shining moon
far out among the heather
I wandered all alone.

Where'er its beams broke through
the branches danced wild shadows
and patterns silver-hued.

For miles no single sound
except a lone owl calling –
then silence all around.

That night of nights the power
of love awoke within me:
I lost my heart that hour.

For her alone I yearned:
if she were only with me
and never from me turned!

Led on by longing's guise
I heard her very footsteps
and looked into her eyes.

What joy beyond compare,
to see her cherished features –
O might it stay fore'er!

to a café on Geist-Strasse and ate something, and then walked
to the moor, where I experienced the most glorious night of
my life, praying and thinking of you." This is the night described
in the poem above. Three days later, on Good Friday (March
29), having received permission from Emmy's parents – though
not his own – the couple was engaged.

Durch Birken schien der Mond
in hellen, weissen Strahlen,
bezaubernd, ungewohnt.

So wird sie wirklich mein?
Du wolltest sie mir geben?
Sie will die Meine sein?

Der dunkle Wald verschwand:
Der Mond bestrahlt die Lichtung,
ein helles, klares Land.

Ich wusste, sie wird mein,
ich war so überglücklich!
Wie konnt' es anders sein?

Halle, März 1907

An Emmy

Es war vor wenig Wochen,
da schaute ich sie an,
und ohn' dass sie gesprochen,
hat sie mir's angetan.

Ich konnt's nicht mehr vergessen,
sie schwebte um mich her.
Ich wag's nicht zu ermessen,
wie fern sie mir noch wär'.

On March 30 (Easter Saturday) Eberhard visited Emmy and
her family and read them the two poems above. Later the same

The moon now cast its bright
white beams upon the birches –
a strange, bewitching sight.

O will she be my own?
To me, Lord, have you giv'n her?
And does she long for me?

The shadows disappeared.
The moon lit up the heather.
The land lay bright and clear.

She will be mine, I know!
My heart is overflowing –
how could it not be so?

Halle, March 1907

To Emmy

'Twas only weeks ago that I
first laid my eyes on her –
and that she stole my heart,
although she never said a word.

How could I *not* remember her?
She hovered in my mind,
though I myself dared not to guess
if she the same would find.

day he left for Breslau, where he planned to seek his parents'
approval of his engagement.

Ich habe nachgesonnen:
Wo find' ich ihre Spur?
O hätt' ich sie gewonnen!
O sähe ich sie nur!

Es hat nicht lang gedauert,
da ist es schon geschehn:
Welch Freud hat mich durchschauert,
als sie mich angesehn!

Und als sie mir gegeben
die süsse, liebe Hand,
da wagte ich zu streben,
bis ich sie gänzlich fand!

Nach tiefem, ernsten Flehen
bei klarem Mondenschein
liess Gott das Wort ergehen:
Sei fröhlich, sie wird dein!

Drei Tage nur vergingen
voll Segens mir und ihr;
der Herr liess es gelingen,
verbunden waren wir!

Wir haben uns erraten:
Ist's möglich, du liebst mich?
Ohn' Worte war's verraten:
Ich liebe einzig dich!

I pondered how to find her,
wondered where her steps might wend.
O could I only win her –
just see her once again!

And it was not long after this
that all my dreams came true.
What happiness transfixed me!
Our eyes locked, and we knew…

It was when she placed in mine
her sweet and lovely hand,
that at last I dared to woo her,
her willing heart to find.

Then came, beneath the moonlight,
after deep and earnest prayers,
God's answer to my waiting heart:
"Rejoice, she will be yours."

Three days passed by, and quickly,
full of blessings for us both,
till, through the Lord, it happened:
we bound ourselves in troth.

And though we'd ask each other,
 "Do you love me? Is it true?"
We knew it plainly, without words:
 "Of course – and only you."

Wer hätt' sich da besonnen?
Ich habe sie gefragt:
Du hast mich lieb gewonnen?
Und sie hat ja gesagt.

Nun gibt es lauter Jubel,
nun lachet Glück und Freud!
Wir haben uns nun wirklich,
in Ewigkeit wie heut!

Halle, März 1907

An Emmy

Emmy, meine süsse Liebe,
du bist mein und ich bin dein!
In des Geistes reinem Triebe
sind wir beide gänzlich Sein!

Sein zu bleiben, ihm zu leben,
ist die Sehnsucht unsres Seins!
Glaubend wir die Augen heben
zu dem Lichtglanz seines Scheins!

Staunend dürfen wir es schauen,
welche Gnade er uns gibt!

Written on Easter Monday and Tuesday, the poem, "Emmy, sweetest gift" reflects Eberhard's exuberance over his engagement to Emmy. He wrote (April 1) "If only I could sit here with Emmy now and talk with her about our wonderful happiness,

And so, no longer tarrying
to claim such happiness,
I asked her if she'd marry me,
and she gave to me her Yes.

And now – what jubilation,
what joy, what bliss, what glee!
For we have one another
now and eternally.

Halle, March 1907

To Emmy

Emmy, sweetest gift of love:
you are mine, and I am yours.
In the pureness of the Spirit,
we belong unto the Lord.

For him living, his remaining –
this is our inmost desire.
Trusting him, we lift our eyes
to meet the radiance of his fire.

In amazement we behold
the endless bounty of his grace.

about Jesus and total dedication to him!" On April 13 he returned to Halle, where he visited the von Hollanders for a
week, and read them this and several other poems one evening
at dinner.

Dürfen seiner Liebe trauen,
die uns ewiglich geliebt!

Freude hat er uns geschüttet
überreich ins volle Herz.
Und, wie's jeder von uns bittet,
richtet er uns himmelwärts!

Jesus nur ist es gewesen,
der uns beide glücklich macht!
Er liess völlig uns genesen.
Nichts als Freude um uns lacht.

Jesus gab uns völl'gen Frieden.
Jesus gab uns ganzes Heil.
Jesus hat uns Glück beschieden,
wie's noch niemand ward zuteil!

Jesus soll es einzig bleiben,
dem wir dienen Tag um Tag!
Nur zu ihm die Herzen treiben,
sein zu bleiben, komm' was mag.

Jesu sind wir fest verschrieben,
unauflöslich, gänzlich Sein!
Weil wir ihn so völlig lieben,
bist du mein, und ich bin dein!

Breslau, 1.– 2. April 1907

We can fully trust his love,
for he has loved us all our days.

From his wealth, the Lord has showered
abundant joy on our full hearts,
and in answer to our prayers
he guides us to him, heavenwards.

It is Jesus Christ alone
who's given us our happiness.
He who banished all our sorrows
smiles with purest joy on us.

Jesus gave us fullest healing,
Jesus gave us perfect peace.
None has known such happiness
as Jesus has on us released.

Jesus is the only master
whom we'll serve from day to day.
Our hearts beat for him alone:
we're his forever, come what may.

Bound in loyalty to Jesus,
pledged to him, unbreakably,
I'm always yours; you, always mine –
because we love him endlessly.

Breslau, April 1–2, 1907

An Emmy

Wir sagen es uns immer wieder:
Die Worte sind uns viel zu arm!
Es schildern nicht die schönsten Lieder,
wie wir empfinden, tief und warm!

Doch ist's nicht nötig, es zu sagen,
wir wissen es auch ohne Wort:
Wir können kaum das Glück ertragen,
das mit uns ist an jedem Ort.

Es strahlt uns überall die Sonne,
die Sonne seiner Lieb' und Gnad'!
Sie gibt uns lauter Freud' und Wonne,
kein dunkler Schatten uns noch naht.

Es muss ja alles Freude werden,
wo Jesus Christus ist der Herr.
Es gibt ein volles Glück auf Erden,
wo er regieret, er, nur er!

Wir haben uns in ihm gefunden,
in ihm, der unser alles ist.
Wir sind so innig tief verbunden,
weil uns vereinte Jesus Christ.

Drum gehn wir freudig seine Stege,
geeint, zusammen Hand in Hand,
verbunden treu auf seinem Wege,
der sicher führt ins bessre Land.

Wir brauchen uns nicht Treu' zu schwören.
Wir wissen es ganz felsenfest,

To Emmy

So often have we noted it –
how little the noblest words reveal.
The sweetest song on earth cannot
describe the deep love that we feel.

And yet, there is no need for speech,
because we know it without a word:
where'er we go, new joy – so great
we scarce can bear it – is assured.

Bright sunlight streams down over us –
the sunlight of God's love and grace
and boundless happiness and joy –
and every shadow is displaced.

Yes, happiness unbroken rules
in every heart that's in accord
with Christ: and so it is on earth
wherever he alone is Lord.

In Jesus Christ, our all and all,
it was that we first sought and found
each other; and in him our love
and unity is sealed and bound.

So we will gladly trace his path
as one, together, hand in hand,
and follow his steps faithfully,
our sure guide to a better land.

We'll swear no oath of loyalty:
with rock-like certainty we know

dass wir uns ganz und stets gehören,
weil seine Hand uns niemals lässt.

Breslau, 7. April 1907

Nach dem Abschied

Ich kann es noch nicht fassen.
Nun ist sie fort von mir!
Wie konnte ich sie lassen?
Das Herz zerreisst es mir!

Oh, kann ich je bezwingen
des Trennungsschmerzes Sturm?
Kann ich ihn niederringen,
ich armer, schwacher Wurm?

Nein, niemals würd' ich fröhlich,
wär' Jesus nicht mein Stern.
In ihm nur sind wir selig,
und wär'n wir noch so fern!

Vor Jesus werd' ich stille.
Mein König kämpft für mich.
Es war sein Gnadenwille.
Er trägt uns mächtiglich!

Ja, Jesu, dir vertrauen
ist volle Seligkeit!

During the Whitsun holidays (May 19–29) Emmy stayed
with Eberhard and his family in Breslau. Afterward, Eberhard
wrote, "When you had gone, I sat at my desk for a long time,
my face in my hands, and could hardly find my way. But I re-

that we belong together fore'er,
that Christ's hand will ne'er let us go.

Breslau, April 7, 1907

After the farewell

I still cannot quite grasp it
that she had to depart.
How could I let it happen?
It tears my very heart!

Could I but only conquer
this storm of parting's pain!
Or can it not be vanquished –
weak worm that I remain?

No, I could ne'er be happy,
were Jesus not my star.
'Tis he gives us contentment,
though far apart we are.

So will I rest in Jesus,
my king. He'll fight for me –
his grace led us together,
he bears us mightily.

Yes, Jesus, this is fullness
of joy: to trust in thee,

ceived strength from our Lord." He wrote the poem above the
same day. On May 30, having received it, Emmy replied, "It made
me endlessly happy. I read it again and again, for I have just the
same longing for you."

Wer glaubt wird freudig schauen
des Heilands Herrlichkeit!

Ich weiss, du führst sie sicher,
die wonnigliche Braut!
Du kennest meine Emmy,
wie ganz sie dir vertraut!

Ich liebe sie so völlig,
dass ich's nicht sagen kann.
Ich bin in ihr so selig,
gehöre ganz ihr an!

Sie ist mein ein und alles
in dir, mein Gott und Herr!
In alle Weiten schall' es:
Ich liebe dich noch mehr!

Je völl'ger ich mich gebe
ganz dir zum Eigentum,
je reiner ich dir lebe
zu deines Namens Ruhm,

ja, um so mehr gehöre
ich ganz der süssen Braut.
Wer nur sucht deine Ehre,
des Glückes Höhen schaut.

Auf dich sind wir verbunden.
Wir schwören nur auf dich!
Hindurch durch alle Stunden
dein eigen ewiglich!

Breslau, 29. Mai 1907

for who believes is blissful
and shall thy glories see.

I know thou'lt lead her surely –
Emmy, my bride-to-be.
Thou knowest how completely
she trusts alone in thee.

So dearly do I love her –
much more than words can say.
With her I'm truly happy.
I shall be hers alway.

She is my own, my dear one,
in thee, my God and Lord.
And yet – far may it echo –
I love thee even more!

The deeper my surrender
to thee, to be thine own –
the purer my heart's striving
to honor thee alone –

the more I am completely
her own in happiness.
For he who praises thee alone
shall see the heights of bliss.

In thee we are united:
we've made our vows on thee.
We're thine for life, each hour –
thine eternally!

Breslau, May 29, 1907

Kampf und Sieg!

Es tost um uns die ernste Schlacht
mit Satans Machtkolonnen.
Drum auf! Gebetet und gewacht!
Der Sieg ist bald gewonnen!

Ein Feldherr führt uns, Jesus Christ,
der keine Schlacht verloren.
Der schwächste Streiter Sieger ist,
da Er den Sieg erkoren!

Die Welt mit ihrer Macht und List
will uns des Muts berauben.
Auf, blicket nur auf Jesus Christ,
mag sie auch Feuer schnauben!

Wir haben nicht mehr Furcht und Angst
trotz Drangsal ohne Massen.
Wenn du nur fest an Jesu hangst,
wird er dich nicht verlassen!

Er ruft dir zu: O sei getrost!
Ich habe überwunden
die Welt, die wütend dich umtost,
in meinen Leidensstunden.

Remembering May–June 1907, Emmy writes in her memoirs that "after Whitsun, and my wonderful time in Breslau… the great fight against Else's conviction…began at home." The bone of contention was Else's announcement on May 8 that

Struggle and victory

Around us in pitched battle
swirl the columns of Satan.
So stand alert, and pray until
the victory is taken.

Our captain is Christ Jesus –
he has never lost a war.
In him the weakest fighter
becomes a conqueror.

The world's deceitful powers
would seek to make us cower,
so keep your eyes on Jesus
despite their fiery glower.

We need not ever be anxious,
though driven without respite.
Hold on, believe in Jesus –
he'll never leave your side.

He calls us now: "Be comforted!
For though the storm still swirls,
through long hours of agony
I have overcome the world."

she intended to receive baptism – an idea popular in the Halle
revival but one bitterly opposed by the von Hollander parents,
who were staunch Lutherans.

Drum Mut! Hier ist ein ganzer Sieg
am Fuss des Marterholzes!
Er, der für uns das Kreuz bestieg,
ward Herr des Satansstolzes!

Nur eins, du musst denselben Tod
zur bitteren Neige kosten!
Du weisst: Er lebt, dein Herr und Gott,
sein Leben wird dich trösten!

Er gibt dir seine Gotteskraft,
ihm gleich zu überwinden!
Der Herr in dir das Wunder schafft,
nur Sieg auf Sieg zu finden!

Breslau, 30. Mai 1907

Dein Auge!

Dein Auge hast du nie geschaut,
den blauen, klaren Stern,
du unvergleichlich schöne Braut,
ich zeigt' ihn dir so gern!

Du weisst, wie ich mich tief versenkt
in deinen klaren Blick!
O hättest du ihn nie gelenkt
von meinem Aug' zurück!

Take heart, for here is victory –
the cross on which Christ died.
He who was martyred for our sake
has crushed the devil's pride.

You, too, must drink the same cup
down to its bitterest dregs,
but know the Lord will comfort you:
his life will be your strength.

He'll gird you with his power,
all evil to overthrow,
and work in you the miracle
to win where'er you go.

Breslau, May 30, 1907

Your eyes

Though you cannot behold your own
fair eyes, my sweetest dear,
I'd show them to you if I could –
they are so blue and clear.

You know how oft I've lost myself
beneath their starry gaze.
O would you never turn from me
and let their brightness fade!

Mir war, als ob ein weites Meer
vor meinem Auge läg',
als ob es lauter Wonne wär',
ohn' Ufer, ohne Steg!

Die Liebe leuchtete so rein
in deinem Augenpaar!
Mir war's, als würf' ich mich hinein,
versänke ganz und gar!

Ja, wenn ich dieses Auge seh',
vergess' ich alles um mich her!
Und mich durchzöge tiefes Weh,
sobald ich ferne wär'!

Doch weiss ich einen einz'gen Weg,
auf dem es sicher ist,
dass stets vor mir dein Auge läg' –
und er heisst Jesus Christ!

Ja, Emmy, richte deinen Stern
nur ganz auf Jesus Christ!
Bei ihm, dem hochgelobten Herrn,
auch stets mein Auge ist!

Breslau, 31. Mai 1907

You look at me, and in my mind
I see an ocean wide –
a boundless sea of pure delight
borne on an endless tide.

The love that your eyes radiate
reflects such clarity –
it seems I could immerse myself
right in it, utterly.

When I see you, all other thoughts
and dreams and plans depart.
As soon as I am far from you,
pain strikes my deepest heart.

I know one way and only one,
which certainty affords
that your eyes will fore'er be mine –
the way of Christ, our Lord.

Yes, Emmy, fix your gaze on him –
on none but Jesus Christ.
On him, our Lord, forever,
I, too, will keep my eyes.

Breslau, May 31, 1907

Auf ewig!

Ich habe sie gefunden,
die eine einz'ge Braut!
Wir haben uns verbunden,
einander ganz vertraut.

Auf weitem Erdenrunde
gibt's keine Seele mehr,
die unserm Herzensbunde
von fern zu nähern wär!

Ja, du bist mein auf ewig!
Und ich bin ewig dein!
So sind wir ewig selig –
es kann nicht anders sein!

So kann kein Tod uns scheiden.
Ich wag' dies ernste Wort.
Es bleibet bei uns beiden
hier wie im Himmel dort!

Sind wir doch fest verbunden
als Jesu Eigentum!
Wir haben uns gefunden
zu unsres Jesu Ruhm!

Breslau, 1. Juni 1907

Eberhard mailed the poem above to Emmy with this note:
"I want to let you know that I am once again happy and joyful
after writing this serious poem (which only you can under-

Forever

I've found her, my beloved,
my one and only bride.
We're bound as one forever,
together, side by side.

There is no other soul on earth
as close to us, or dear,
as we are to each other:
our loyalty is clear.

Yes, you are mine forever,
and I am truly yours,
forever blest and happy –
no other way is ours.

E'en death shall not part us –
I dare this solemn vow.
Our love will stand forever,
in heaven, as here and now.

For we are firmly bound
in Jesus, as his own.
In him we've found each other –
all praise be his alone.

Breslau, June 1, 1907

stand) and after surrendering myself and you in full trust to
Jesus' glorious leading."

Trost und Freude!

Nun ist sie fern von mir!
Doch sind die Herzen nah!
Was ich durchlebe hier,
in ihr bald auch geschah!

So sind wir völlig einig,
in eins verschmolzen ganz,
du mein und ich ganz deinig,
du, meines Lebens Kranz!

Schwer hab ich dich vermisst!
Doch bald brach durch der Stern:
Uns führet Jesus Christ!
Wir haben doch den Herrn!

Die Freude macht uns stille.
Ja, ihm vertrauen wir!
Zum Besten führt sein Wille,
bei dir wie auch bei mir!

Erst war mir bang und weh,
doch bald so frei und froh!
Im Geiste dich ich seh':
Du fühlst ja ebenso!

So sind wir immer fröhlich!
Wir sind uns niemals fern.
Wir wissen uns so selig
in unserm treuen Herrn!

Comfort and joy

You're far from me right now,
and yet our hearts are tuned
so that whate'er I think and feel
strikes your heart, too, and soon.

> Yes, we are truly welded
> together, closely bound:
> I'm yours, and you are mine alone –
> you are my life's true crown.

How sorely do I miss you,
and yet, there shines our star:
Jesus Christ, our leader
and Lord – he's never far.

> Our joy sets us at rest.
> We've given him our trust
> and know the path he has in mind
> is best for both of us.

First I was sad and anxious,
yet now I'm glad and free.
I see you now in my mind's eye
and know you feel like me.

> So we'll always stay joyful
> held close, in one accord,
> and know our happiness and bliss
> is grounded in the Lord.

Wie sehnt' ich mich so sehr!
Doch nun genügt es mir:
Du liebst mich mehr und mehr,
und ich gehöre dir!

Ganz glücklich sind wir beide,
denn uns gehören wir,
in Freuden wie im Leide,
ich dir und du ganz mir!

Breslau, 2. Juni 1907

Ihre Seele!

Die Tiefen ihrer Seele
such' ich mit ganzer Kraft.
Ihr Herz ich ganz erwähle.
Ihr Sinn mir Frieden schafft.

O könnt' ich je ergründen
ihr herrlich edles Herz,
ihr Tiefstes völlig finden,
so stürb' der Sehnsucht Schmerz.

O könnt' ich gleichsam trinken
ihr ganzes Denken, Tun!
O könnte ich versinken,
in ihrer Tiefe ruhn!

How ardent was my longing!
Yet now I am content.
Your love for me is boundless,
and I'm yours without end.

Yes, we belong together,
and our joy is sublime.
In happiness or sorrow,
I'm yours – you're fully mine.

Breslau, June 2, 1907

Her soul

I've sought with all I have
to know her inmost soul –
her being gives me peace;
to win her is my goal.

O could I ever fathom
her lovely, noble heart
and know her deepest feelings –
my pain would then depart.

Could I but drink in everything –
all that she thinks and does –
and lose myself within her,
find rest there, and repose!

Oh, dass ich alle Züge,
die ihre Seele trägt,
in meinem Herzen trüge,
von ihr hineingelegt!

Breslau, 9. Juni 1907

Dennoch Sieg!

Die Sünde fasst das schwache Herz,
Versuchung nahet überall!
Der Satan schürt den bittren Schmerz:
Ist Leben Fall auf Fall?

Aus trübem, dunklem Grund ersteht
des Zweifels furchtbar fragend Wort:
Ist neues Leben hier gesät,
wo Sünden leben fort und fort?

O Seele, was hat er gesagt?
Sollst du das neue Leben sein?
Wo wäre der, der nicht verzagt –
sollt' seine Seel' so werden rein?

Nein, Jesus ist des Lebens Brot!
O halleluja, er dir lebt!

In the letter that enclosed the poem above, Eberhard told Emmy, "I think you brood too much and look much too much into yourself. Today's poem will tell you what I mean…Nothing but looking toward Jesus can give deliverance and certainty. Clearly we must put up a fight against every sinful impulse, and

Then might each trait, each feature
that her pure soul adorns,
imparted in me by her,
by my own soul be borne.

Breslau, June 9, 1907

Still victorious

Sin grasps and holds the wavering heart.
Temptation looms and threatens all.
Satan inflames the smarting wound:
is life a trap – fall after fall?

From drear, dark depths awakes a sigh –
the gnawing fear of questioning doubt.
Can new life spring up here, be sown
where sin is still not rooted out?

My soul, what does the Father want?
This cannot be the life he means!
For how could any resist despair,
had he to wash his own soul clean?

No, Christ alone is the bread of life.
Cry out for joy: he is your light!

we cannot do this earnestly enough. But, my little dove, we must not remain downcast…Always joyful and happy – that is how I want you to be! There are so few Christians who are like that. Though reborn, they do not understand the victory of looking toward Christ, but keep gazing within."

Nicht dein, nein, Jesu Kreuzestod
dein Herz auf seine Höhen hebt!

Drum auf! Mit frohem Glaubensblick
auf Jesus ganz allein geschaut!
Wir blicken niemals mehr zurück,
wir haben nur auf ihn gebaut!

In uns ist alles hohl und schlecht,
nur seine Kraft ist herrlich, hehr.
Wen Jesus frei macht, ist es recht,
nur stark in ihm, vom Eignen leer.

Breslau, 16. Juni 1907

Reiner Dienst

Herr, höre meine eine Bitte
aus ganzem Herzen dir gesagt:
Lass jeden meiner Glaubensschritte
zu deiner Ehre sei gewagt!

Ich weiss, du wirkest mächt'ge Taten
durch mich, wie jeden, der da glaubt.
Zur Ernte stehen weite Saaten,
dem Feinde ist der Sieg geraubt!

Doch, Herr, gib heilig reinen Segen!
Das Ich lass ganz im Tode sein!

In a letter he sent Emmy with "Pure service," Eberhard wrote, "I find praise harder to take than blame and misunder-

Not your death, but his on the cross
shall bear you upward to his heights.

Then up, and look with eyes of faith
and steadfast joy on him alone.
Take not another backward glance
from Jesus, your life's cornerstone.

Within us all is dark and void –
his strength alone should be adored.
Whom Jesus frees is truly freed –
empty of self, strong in the Lord.

Breslau, June 16, 1907

Pure service

Lord, I beg thee from my heart –
hear and heed this single plea:
let every step of faith I venture
count alone as honor to thee.

I've seen what great deeds thou canst work
through me and anyone who trusts.
Whole fields stand ready for thy harvest –
fields the Foe has surely lost.

But grant me, Lord, a purer blessing:
let the self be put to death.

standing, because it is tempting. I give thanks for being slighted
and misunderstood…because it is good for me to be humbled."

Lass alle Brüder niederlegen
vor dir die Ehre ganz allein!

Ja, Herr, dies eine musst du geben:
für mich auch keinen Schatten Ruhm!
Nur dir, nur dir, mein armes Leben,
zu deinem Preis dein Eigentum!

Ertöte du die Menschensünde,
die dir die heil'ge Ehre raubt,
dass niemand mehr die Kühnheit finde
zu ehren den, der nur geglaubt!

Erweise du in heil'ger Klarheit,
wie elend Menschen vor dir sind.
Wie ferne ist von deiner Wahrheit,
wer da den Grund des Segens find't.

Vernichte alle Menschenehre
durch deine heil'ge Majestät!
So mächtig dich dein Geist verkläre,
dass aller Menschenruhm verweht!

Breslau, 21. Juni 1907

May every child of thine give praise
to thee alone with every breath.

Grant me, Lord, this one request:
guard me from any hint of fame.
Poor as it is, my life is thine
and ought to glorify thy name.

Destroy the sin of men who'd steal
the honor that belongs to thee.
Let no one dare to praise another
who simply listened – and believed.

Lord, show me with thy clarity
how poor all men are in thy sight,
and how success so quickly leads them
far away from truth and light.

Stamp out all human praise, and show
the fullness of thy majesty.
Reveal thy Spirit with such power
that all who honor men must flee.

Breslau, June 21, 1907

Unsere Liebe!

Es ist nicht lang, da überflog
ein süsses Lächeln ihr Gesicht,
und wie sie's auch zur Seite bog,
verbergen konnte sie es nicht.

Dies Lächeln sagte mir so viel!
Es war unsagbar lieblich, süss!
Verriet so zart, wie ihr gefiel,
was meine Liebe merken liess!

Dann kam der Tag, da gab sie mir
den ersten Kuss – so lieblich bang.
Ja, Ebbo, ich gehöre dir!
In Jesus ich an dir nur hang'!

O Emmy, wie ist unsre Liebe
seit dieser Zeit entflammt so hoch!
Wie glühen unsrer Herzen Triebe
stets reiner, wahrer, tiefer noch!

Jetzt kann ich's nicht mehr zählen, nennen,
wie deine Liebe mich beglückt.
Je mehr ich durfte dich erkennen,
je tiefer hast du mich beglückt!

Noting that it was three months since they had been engaged, Eberhard sent this poem to Emmy with a letter, in which he wrote, "I must tell you how terribly much – how enormously – I love you, so much so that I am yours with every fiber of my being, with each and every thought. Yet in all my longing I am utterly at peace, because we belong so completely to one another and are so very happy in Him!" Later in the

Our love

Not long ago I chanced to notice
how she quickly turned aside.
A fleeting smile had lit her face –
she could not hide it, though she tried.

This gesture said so much to me,
for it was sweet beyond compare,
and by it she betrayed her joy
and gladness in my love for her.

Soon after this, the day came
when she gave me her first bashful kiss,
saying, "Ebbo, I belong to you –
in Jesus, for we are both his."

O Emmy: how our love has grown
since then, and flared up ever higher!
And how each impulse of our hearts
glows with a stronger, purer fire!

I can no longer count the ways
that your love brings me happiness,
for the more I learn about you,
the greater, deeper is my bliss.

same letter, in reference to his ongoing struggle to find clarity
with regard to adult (versus infant) baptism, he writes, "My po-
sition has become clearer. Stimulated by the text you sent…
and thinking about our possible baptism, and of the persecu-
tions of the end times, I drafted the enclosed poem. Afterward
I rode to a quiet wood to reflect about it and to pray."

Und nicht allein dein süsses Wesen
hat tief dich lieben mich gelehrt;
nein, deine Seele durft' ich lesen.
Dies höchste Glück hast du gewährt!

O Emmy, völlig dich erkennen
ist meiner Seele tiefer Drang.
Ich darf ja mein dich gänzlich nennen;
an dir allein ich ewig hang'!

Breslau, 29. Juni 1907

Falsche Freundschaft und wahre Liebe

O Emmy, als ich dich nicht kannte,
noch nie in deine Augen sah,
eh' Gott mir deine Liebe sandte,
so vieles Dunkle mir geschah!

Manch' Düstres war in meinem Leben!
Nur er, mein Jesus, war mein Trost.
Nur seine Gnade konnt' mich heben,
so oft in mir der Kampf getost.

Viel Dunkelheit und bittre Täuschung
griff schmerzend in mein Leben ein.
Es wirkten manche arme Menschen
verwirrend, drückend auf mich ein.

Before meeting Emmy, Eberhard had befriended another young woman. He was open with Emmy about this from the start of their relationship, but continued to be plagued by regrets, as "False friendship" shows. He sent it to Emmy on July 3,

'Twas not alone your nature sweet
that deepened my first love for you.
You gave me joy in greater treasure:
your inmost soul you showed me, too.

And that, dear Emmy – to know your heart
completely – is my deepest plea:
to call you mine without reserve,
and stay with you eternally.

Breslau, June 29, 1907

False friendship and true love

Emmy, long before I knew you,
or ever looked into your face,
before God led me to your love –
my life was dark and without grace.

Such melancholy marked my days!
Jesus was my only balm.
When battles tossed my weary heart,
his grace uplifted me, brought calm.

Darkness, bitter disappointment,
pain and worry weighed me down.
The need of many I encountered
confused me, brought me to the ground.

1907. The next day, she wrote to him, "Your last poem is very
sad. Please, I ask you, be happy!" – to which he responded by
sending the next poem, "Emmy, you alone."

Oft konnte ich den Weg nicht finden:
Oh, wie entflieh' ich dieser Qual?
Wie Sklaven ihre Ketten binden,
befreit' mich nicht die eigne Wahl!

Als dann dein klares blaues Auge
mein Herz erfüllt' mit Himmelsglück,
erkannt' ich völlig, wie nichts tauge,
was hinten lag, so weit zurück!

Nun konnte mich kein Irrlicht täuschen,
es ward mir in den Grund verhasst.
Wenn hell und klar die Sonne leuchtet,
des Nachtlichts Schimmer bald verblasst.

Die falsche Freundschaft ward gebrochen,
gelöst in Ruhe, ohne Hast.
Was ich erbeten viele Wochen,
ich war befreit von ihrer Last!

Die Ketten sind nun ganz verschwunden,
für immer ganz in Staub verweht!
Im klaren Licht, das ich gefunden,
das Unrecht unverborgen steht.

O Emmy, lass uns ganz vergessen,
in Jesu, dieses dunkle Blatt!
Wir können niemals doch ermessen,
wie schwer die Schuld gewogen hat.

How often the way ahead seemed barred!
Yet try as I might to flee my misery,
I found – a slave bound by his chain –
my own choice could not set me free.

'Twas when I saw your clear, blue eyes
that my heart brimmed with joy at last,
and that I saw the worthlessness
of all that had filled me in the past.

No more could a mirage mislead me:
I hated falsehood with all my heart.
Sunlight shone with dazzling brightness –
night's pale glimmer must depart.

So were false friendship's bonds undone,
not with haste, but quietly.
After long weeks of prayer I was
at last unburdened and set free.

Gone are the chains that held me fast,
fallen to dust and swept away.
Evil is powerless, once it stands
uncovered in the light of day.

Then let us completely put aside,
in Jesus, the darkness of past days.
In any case, no man can know
the breadth of his guilt, or what it weighs.

Der Herr hat alles ganz vergeben,
getilgt ist alles durch sein Blut.
Stets reiner will ich Jesu leben,
und ganz vertrauen seiner Hut!

Und du, mein Glück und meine Wonne,
oh, deine Liebe ist ja mein!
Du meines Lebens Freudensonne,
für immer bin ich einzig dein!

Breslau, 3. Juli 1907

Emmy, nur dich
einzig lieb' ich!

Emmy, nur dir
atme ich hier!

Emmy, nur du
meine ewige Ruh'!

Emmy, auch wir
des Heilandes Zier!

Breslau, 4. Juli 1907

The Lord's forgiven all – his blood
has wiped away our sins fore'er.
I'll live more purely now in him
and trust in his protecting care.

And you – what happiness and bliss! –
just as your love belongs to me,
O sun who fills my life with joy,
I will be yours eternally.

Breslau, July 3, 1907

Emmy, you alone,
no other, do I love.

Emmy, for you
alone do I breathe.

Emmy, you alone –
my endless repose.

Emmy, together
we're the Savior's own.

Breslau, July 4, 1907

Halleluja!

Die Last ist fort! Ich jauchze laut:
Mein Jesus hat vergeben!
Durch ihn hat meine einz'ge Braut
das Glück mir neu gegeben.

O Überwinder aller Not,
du Fürst des Herzensfriedens!
Du gabst dem Kummer seinen Tod.
Ich bin von ihm geschieden!

Die Sünde ist hinweggetan.
Dein Friede nun regieret.
Ich gehe fröhlich meine Bahn.
Wer dich hat, triumphieret!

Breslau, 5. Juli 1907

Und dieser Quell des Lebens,
für dich er fließet heut.
Dein Jesus ist dein König,
sein Wille deine Freud'!

Breslau, 8.–9. Juli 1907

Finally relieved of any lingering guilt (see previous note) Eberhard wrote the poem "Hallelujah!" and sent it to Emmy. She replied the next day, "Your happy poem gives me much joy. You are right: in God's presence is fullness of joy. The Lord overwhelms us."

Hallelujah!

My burden's gone! I will rejoice,
for Jesus has forgiven me,
and through him, my beloved one
has brought new happiness to me.

O conqueror of all distress,
O prince who fills my heart with peace,
you gave the deathblow to my grief
and granted me complete release!

All sin is banished, swept away.
I travel onward joyously,
and in my heart your peace holds sway,
for who knows you, knows victory.

Breslau, July 5, 1907

This spring of living water
flows down to you today
from Christ, your king, whose will
shall be your joy always.

Breslau, July 8–9, 1907

Eberhard wrote "This spring of living water" on the back of a
postcard "around 1 o'clock at night"; the front is a painting of a
mountain waterfall.

Liebe und Wahrheit

Die Welt hat lauter Lügen,
in jedem Freudenbecher Gift!
Der Stärkste muss betrügen,
der abwärts mit dem Strome schifft!

Man spricht so viel von Liebe,
doch hat man nie sie wahr gefühlt.
Es bleiben Lügentriebe,
ein jeder vielerlei verhüllt.

Nur Er, Er ist die Wahrheit!
Vor ihm liegt alles offen da.
Die Seinen wollen Klarheit!
Sie hassen, was das Licht nicht sah!

So gibt es eine Liebe,
von aller Art von Lüge frei,
in heilig reinem Triebe
ganz offen, sei es, was es sei!

So, Emmy, wir uns lieben!
Bei uns ist alles klar.
Ja, jede Scheu vertrieben,
nur Liebe, ganz und gar!

After telling Emmy in a letter (July 7) how hard he had found it to be open with her about his past, he added, "Yet I am terribly glad I did it, for I am so free and happy now! I will always tell you everything of any importance…even if it is very hard for both of us. There is no need for us to burden each other with minor difficulties that are quickly resolved. But I expect to know

Love and truth

The world is full of lies –
there's poison in each cup of joy.
In following the current,
the strongest use dishonest ploys.

There's endless talk of love,
but few have truly felt its touch.
Falsehood lurks in each of us –
we cover, hide, and mask so much.

Yes, God alone is truth,
and all is open to his sight.
His followers seek clarity
and hate what's hidden from the light.

His love alone's untainted,
free from every kind of lie –
an impulse, pure and holy:
sincere and honest, without guise.

So is our love, dear Emmy.
Between us all is clear and plain.
All shyness now has vanished.
Love, and love alone, remains.

absolutely everything about my fiancée that is a burden for her,
and she should be able to expect the same of me." Replying the
next day, Emmy agreed: "I find it absolutely necessary, as you do,
that we tell each other everything. I think it is a disgrace when an
engaged couple lie to each other, as happens so often."

Wir sind darin so selig:
Mein Liebchen alles weiss!
Das macht uns immer fröhlich,
so ist kein Kampf zu heiss!

Wir wollen alles tragen,
und wenn's das Schwerste wär',
wir wollen es uns sagen!
So gibt's kein' Kummer mehr!

Und alle unsre Freude
wird tausendmal so gross,
wenn wir sie wissen beide;
das Glück ist grenzenlos.

Breslau, 9. Juli 1907

Überall Jesus!

Die Liebe Jesu mit uns geht
wohin wir immer gehen.
Der Heiland uns zur Seite steht,
lässt Seine Gnad' uns sehen!

Er ist bei uns mit ganzer Kraft.
Er lässt uns immer siegen!
Sein Segen neue Kräfte schafft,
dass nie wir unterliegen!

Eberhard wrote "Jesus everywhere!" for Emmy on the eve of her move to Salzwedel, a parish where she was to take up quarters with a pastor's family as a nurse for the children. In the letter he sent with the poem, Eberhard writes, "May God bless you in Salzwedel! I rejoice that the Lord wants to use you as a

In this we are both blissful:
that we share every joy and grief.
Yes, we'll be happy always –
no fight we face will be too fierce.

We'll carry every burden,
however hard it is to bear,
and tell each other everything,
thus banishing each lingering care.

So will love's joys and blessings
increase for us a thousand fold,
and both of us shall share
in boundless happiness untold.

Breslau, July 9, 1907

Jesus everywhere!

The love of Jesus goes with us
where'er we may be going.
The Savior stands beside us,
his loving mercy showing.

In victory after victory,
he gives us his full powers.
He blessings bring new energy.
Defeat is never ours.

blessing to all…from the old lady to the little children to Herr
Pastor. I have always found that the more joyfully and naturally,
the more freely and simply we go on our way – if we are serious about giving over all we are and have to Jesus – the more
certain and glorious the victory will be!"

EBERHARD ARNOLD

Sein Friede ist an jedem Ort
in allen, die ihm trauen.
Ja, Jesus, unser Freudenhort,
führt uns auf Friedensauen.

Wohin wir kommen, überall
ist Jesus unser Leben.
An jedem Ort sein Lob erschall!
Zu ihm wir uns erheben.

Der Christen Lauf ein Siegeslauf,
ein stetes Freudenleben!
O kommet alle, kommt zuhauf,
um Jesus Preis zu geben!

Breslau, 11. Juli 1907

Tod und Rettung

Die Menschheit liegt in tiefer Nacht,
beherrscht von finsterer Gewalt.
Es ist des dunklen Abgrunds Macht
in tückisch furchtbarer Gestalt.

Die Sünde ist der Menschheit Fluch
in schwerer Last als Todesbann.
Der Hölle tötend Pestgeruch
vergiftet schleichend Kind und Mann.

Explaining the impetus for "Death and salvation" – an unpleasant family scene with his parents, who were increasingly exasperated about his growing disregard for convention and his continued questioning of such practices as infant baptism –

His peace is there for everyone –
for all those who believe.
Yes, Jesus is our source of joy,
leads us to fields of peace.

Christ Jesus is our very life
no matter where we are,
so let us raise our hearts to him
and shout his praise afar!

The Christian's life is always
a victorious, joyful race.
So come, ye throngs, to Jesus,
and give him all your praise.

Breslau, July 11, 1907

Death and salvation

Ruled by murky powers of gloom,
whole peoples languish, deep in night,
bound by dread and dark deceit –
held by an abysmal might.

The curse of humankind is sin;
its final blow, the sting of death
that poisons every man or child
who breathes its pestilential breath.

Eberhard wrote to Emmy (July 14) that it had given him "a shat-
tering glimpse into people's servitude to sin…I must designate
sin as sin and have nothing to do with it. And I must talk with
Mama about her soul. Oh, that she might be saved!"

Mit grausig fürchterlicher Kraft
beherrscht die Sünde jeden Sinn.
Den Stärksten raubt sie Mark und Saft,
so haltlos taumeln sie dahin.

O dringt uns nicht die Todesnot
verlorner Menschen um uns her,
zu flehen heiss zu unserm Gott,
dass Jesus dem Verderben wehr'?

Wir fühlen tief den heissen Drang
zu retten, was zu retten ist,
zu sprengen froh des Teufels Zwang
durch unsern Retter Jesus Christ.

Drum auf zum Kampf mit Nacht und Tod!
Es lodre heller unser Licht!
Gebrochen ist der Sünde Not,
vor Jesus bleibt das Böse nicht!

Breslau, 12. Juli 1907

Lauter Freude!

Friede, Freude, lauter Jubel
hat unser Jesus uns gebracht,
überströmend Freudenstrudel!
Der volle Friede um uns lacht!

Strained relations at home (see previous note) only heightened Eberhard's love for Emmy, as the poem "Pure joy" shows.

With grasping, cruel, and fearsome power
sin holds dominion o'er each sense.
It robs the strongest of their vigor
and leaves them to stumble, blind and dense.

O when we meet such souls, and see
the mortal anguish of their state,
must we not beg God fervently
that Jesus save them from certain fate?

From deep within we feel compelled
to rescue every wavering soul –
with joy help break the devil's chains,
through Christ, who came to make us whole.

Then up, to conquer night and death!
Bright burning brand, flare ever higher!
Sin's grief and pain are broken now –
no evil can withstand Christ's fire.

Breslau, July 12, 1907

Pure joy

Peace and joy and jubilation
flood through us from Jesus Christ,
whirling streams of glad elation –
peace laughs loud on every side.

He sent it to her immediately after writing it, "with deep joy in
my heart."

Jauchze laut, geliebtes Wesen!
Gib die Freude frei heraus!
Nichts als Glück hat er erlesen,
aller Kummer ist nun aus.

Jedem gib die Freude weiter,
wer dir auch entgegentritt!
Du, die Sonne strahlend heiter,
gibst ihm deine Strahlen mit.

Oh, so bald ich wieder sehe
dein einzig herrlich Augenpaar!
Bald, ja bald ich vor dir stehe,
so glücklich wie ich immer war!

Tage dauert's, und ich sehe
mein reines, tiefes Lebensglück,
wenn ich dir zur Seite gehe,
du jeden Kuss mir gibst zurück.

Lass uns, Emmy, diese Wochen
stets strahlend, glücklich, heiter sein!
Jesus hat uns Glück versprochen,
sein Friede lässt uns nie allein.

Breslau, 14. Juli 1907

Sing exulting, my beloved,
radiate your joy to all.
Joy – pure joy – is what Christ offers:
all our sorrows are no more.

Share your happiness with others,
pass it on to everyone.
You, my cheerful, beaming sunshine –
send your rays to all who come.

Soon I shall again be gazing
deep into your lovely eyes.
Soon I shall once more be with you –
greater joy could not be mine.

Only days keep us apart now,
my life's deepest joy and bliss –
then you'll walk along beside me
and return my every kiss.

All our lives let us be joyful,
radiant, happy in the Lord.
Jesus promises his blessings –
peace is ours forevermore.

Breslau, July 14, 1907

Jauchze, singe,
Wonneherz!
Juble, springe,
frei von Schmerz!

Nah dich wissend,
ach so bald
glücklich küssend
fest ich halt!

Jubel, Wonne,
Friedenskind,
Freudensonne,
dich ich find'!

Breslau, 21. Juli 1907

In rüttelndem Zuge
in rasendem Fluge
trotz nahendem Kuß
noch einmal ein Gruß!

3. oder 4. August 1907

Writing on July 21, and enclosing the poem, "Rejoice and sing," Eberhard told Emmy that "at this moment I have only one wish: that you are just as happy as I am." Later in the same letter he rejoices at the thought of meeting her in two weeks' time:

Rejoice and sing,
dearest heart!
Leap with joy,
let sorrow part!

I'll see you soon
again at last,
kiss you happily,
hold you fast.

Child of peace,
of bright sunshine,
of joy and bliss –
you are mine!

Breslau, July 21, 1907

I'm coming at top speed
on a lurching stampede
toward our next kiss –
but I'll still send you this.

August 3 or 4, 1907

"What happy, glorious hours those will be!" So, apparently, were
the hours he spent on the train getting there – see the quatrain
above, which he wrote on the back of a postcard.

Dem Lamme nach!

Dem Lamme nach! O süße Emmy,
wir fürchten uns nun nimmermehr.
Sein Weg führt sicher uns zum Ziele,
und zürnt der Feind auch noch so sehr.

Dem Lamme nach! Welch tiefe Einheit,
nur ihm zu trauen ganz allein,
ihm folgen treu in seiner Reinheit,
sein Eigen, ewig, völlig Sein!

Dem Lamme nach! Welch mächt'ge Stärke!
Von ihm geführet Schritt für Schritt,
durch schwerstes Leid, die grössten Werke,
trägt seine Kraft uns beide mit.

Dem Lamme nach! Welch tiefe Freude,
auf seinem Weg geeint zu gehn,
im frohen Jauchzen wie im Leide
ganz fest und treu bei ihm zu stehn!

Dem Lamme nach! Welch süsser Friede,
auf ihm zu ruhen, selig, still,
stets preisend ihn in Wort und Liede,
ihm lebend, ganz wie er es will!

In the letter he sent with this poem, Eberhard informs Emmy that he has reached "a serious, momentous decision that will have grave consequences and give our life a sharply defined direction, fraught with suffering." After grappling with the question of baptism for four months, he now felt that "scripture recognizes only one baptism, the baptism of those who have become believers. I therefore regard myself as unbaptized and

Follow the Lamb!

Follow the Lamb! My sweetest Emmy,
never again shall we know fear.
His way shall lead us onward surely,
e'en though the furious foe is near.

Follow the Lamb! How deep our oneness
when we trust in him alone
and follow faithfully his pureness,
eternally to be his own!

Follow the Lamb! How powerfully
he guides us on at every step!
Through deepest pain, through greatest effort
we are carried by his strength.

Follow the Lamb! How deep the joy
of going his way hand in hand.
In exultation as in sorrow
faithful at his side we stand.

Follow the Lamb! How sweet our peace
when we rest in him, serene and still,
in word and song forever praising
him, and living by his will!

hereby declare war on the existing church systems…It is, of
course, my wish to be baptized as soon as possible and to leave
the established church." In 1970, for the 50th anniversary of
the founding of the Bruderhof, Marlys Swinger set the poem to
music; it was first sung at a joint brotherhood conference at
Woodcrest in June of that year.

Dem Lamme nach! Welch sel'ges Hoffen
auf jene einz'ge Herrlichkeit!
Geschwunden, was uns einst betroffen.
Wir preisen ihn in Ewigkeit!

Breslau, 4. September 1907

Auf zum Kampf!

Heilig hat der Herr gegeben
eine gläubige Gemein,
einzig ihm als Braut zu leben,
abgesondert Sein zu sein.

Satan, dieser Fürst der Lügen,
hat das Werk des Herrn gestört,
um in Mischmasch umzubiegen,
was doch einzig ihm gehört.

Doch die Wahrheit bleibt untödlich,
und der Glaube lebet noch.
Die Gemeinde bleibet göttlich,
und die Reinheit sieget doch.

Auf zum Kampf, ihr Gottesstreiter!
Weicht der Lüge nimmermehr!

Reflecting on his vision of a true church, and his determina-
tion to fight against worldly distortions, Eberhard indicated to
Emmy (September 16) that he was especially taken with the
ideal described in I Cor. 1:2, 2 Cor. 1:1, and Gal. 1:2. He en-

Follow the Lamb! How blest our hope
in the dawn of that all-glorious Day!
What oppressed us has now vanished –
forevermore we'll sing his praise!

Breslau, September 4, 1907

To battle!

God in holy love has built
a faithful church, his very own,
and chosen her, a cherished bride –
set apart as his alone.

Satan, prince of lies, has sought
to turn this work into his gain,
to mix with evil and distort
what is solely God's domain.

Yet the truth can not be murdered.
Faith is still alive in us.
The church shall be God's own forever,
purity shall rule his house.

Rise up, fighters for God's spirit!
Nevermore give way to lies.

closed the poem, "To battle!" as an expression of his thoughts
on the matter. Marianne Zimmermann set it to music at the
Alm Bruderhof in March 1936, for Heini and Annemarie's wedding, when, she says, "it acquired special meaning for us."

Dringet vorwärts, schreitet weiter,
tobt der Feind auch noch so sehr!

Fleht vom Herrn den Blick der Wahrheit,
dass die Täuschung fallen muss!
Schaut der heil'gen Schriften Klarheit,
lasst uns sein aus einem Guss!

Seht im Wort die scharfe Scheidung:
Nur der Glaube hat den Herrn,
nur der Glaube seine Leitung,
ohne ihn nicht Schal' noch Kern.

Beuget nie mehr eure Knie
einem falschen Gottesdienst!
Dass doch keiner Hilfe sehe
schnöder Täuschung zum Gewinnst.

Auf zum Kampf mit aller Lüge,
gegen Satans Lichtgestalt,
dass die Wahrheit völlig siege
und der Herr erscheine bald!

Auf zum Kampf in voller Einheit,
fort mit allem Sektengeist!
Der Gemeinde klare Reinheit
keine Macht zu Boden reisst.

Breslau, 15. September 1907

Press on forward, do not falter,
though the Foe in fury flies.

Pray for eyes to see the truth.
May all lies be stripped of force.
May God's word give clarity
and make us one – poured from one source.

The word of God brings sharp discernment.
By faith alone can God be known,
and faith alone reveals his leading.
Without his seed, naught can be grown.

Bend your knees no more to idols,
stop all worship of false gods.
Let no one be misled to turn
for help from profiteers of fraud.

Join the fight against all falsehood –
Satan's cunning guise of light –
until truth shall fully conquer,
and the Lord appear in might.

Rise and fight in perfect union.
Cast away all that divides.
Nothing can tear down the church:
its radiant purity e'er abides.

Breslau, September 15, 1907

Aus der Schwäche die Kraft

O Herr, du hast mir neu bewiesen,
wie arm und ohne Kraft ich bin.
So sei dein Blut allein gepriesen!
Nimm mich so bloss und elend hin.

Ja, Herr, du hast mir neu zerbrochen
das Bauen auf die eigne Kraft.
Auf sie will ich nie wieder pochen,
da Menschenkraft nur Kummer schafft.

So lass mich einzig dir vertrauen,
du König Jesus! Siegesfürst!
Dann muss ich Sieg auf Siege schauen,
da du doch triumphieren wirst!

So will ich jubelnd vorwärts schreiten.
Der Sieg ist mein in Ewigkeit.
Du willst mich fest hindurch geleiten.
Wo du bist, ist kein Herzeleid. Amen.

Breslau, 17. September 1907

On September 18, Eberhard received a letter from Emmy's
father in response to their recent decision to be re-baptized.
Passing on news of its arrival to Emmy the same day, he told

Out of weakness, strength

Lord, thou hast shown me once again
my poverty and powerlessness.
For this I praise thy saving blood.
Accept me in my wretchedness.

Lord, thou hast shattered once again
all confidence in my own strength.
No more shall I rely on it –
it only brings regret at length.

Jesus, princely conqueror,
help me trust alone in thee,
who leadeth every fight I enter
to triumphant victory.

So will I stride ahead, exulting,
eternal victory to gain.
I know that thou wilt firmly guide me.
Where thou art, is no more pain.

Breslau, September 17, 1907

her that though her father had assured him that their personal
relationship would remain unchanged, he had also stipulated
the following: there would be no wedding until Eberhard had

Unser Halt

Menschenstützen halten nicht.
Du, Herr, bist uns ganz genug.
Jesus bleibt, wenn alles bricht.

Manche Dunkel um uns sind,
doch der Herr ist unser Licht.
Friede ruht auf seinem Kind.

Manche Schmerzen tragen wir.
Jesus ist's, der Heilung find't.
Heiland, wir vertrauen dir.

Dir wir folgen, frei von Hast.
Deine Ruh' bleibt unsre Zier,
Golgatha, des Herzens Rast.

Jesus Christus bei uns ist:
tief versenkt die Sorgenlast,
überwunden Satans List.

Jesus sagt uns: Freuet euch,
wenn um mich ihr leiden müsst.
Euer ist das Himmelreich.

Jesus, ja, wir folgen dir!
Deine Freude macht uns reich.
Dein für ewig bleiben wir.

Breslau, 19. September 1907

completed his first state examination in theology; the couple
could correspond "only twice a week"; Emmy would have to

Our mainstay

Human props must fall away:
Savior, we need thee alone.
Worlds may break, but thou wilt stay.

Though the darkness may increase,
thou, O Lord, art our true light.
On us, thy children, rests thy peace.

Pain and sorrow weigh on us,
yet we know that thou canst heal.
Thus in thee alone we trust.

Thee we follow, free of haste.
Thy quiet calm remains our help,
Golgotha, our heart's true rest.

Jesus, thou art at our side.
Thou hast cast our burdens far,
Satan's might forever defied.

Thou didst say, "Rejoice, take heart.
All who suffer for my sake
in my kingdom shall take part."

Christ, we would thy followers be,
rich in joy that comes from thee,
thine for all eternity.

Breslau, September 19, 1907

wait one year before being re-baptized; and all visits were off
for one year.

So rot wie Glut
in frischem Duft
die Zeichen meiner Liebe!
Dir pocht mein Blut!
Du Himmelsluft!
Du Sehnsucht aller Triebe!

Breslau, für den 29. September 1907

Jesu Licht!

Ich sehe zwei Birken
sich küssend im Licht.
Es hält sie Sein Wirken
umschlossen so dicht.

So, Emmy, wir beide
umflossen von Licht,
in Freud' und in Leide
umschlungen so dicht.

Breslau, 30. Oktober 1907

Reminding Emmy that they had now been engaged for ex-
actly six months, Eberhard sent her a bouquet of roses with the
verse at the top of this spread.

As if the injunction against meeting for a whole year were
not enough, both Eberhard and Emmy faced other difficulties
with their families in the fall of 1907, and Eberhard was increasingly weighed down by tensions among the leaders of the Ger-

Red as a fire,
fragrant and fresh,
these roses are love's token.
Yes, my heart pounds
for you, heaven's breath.
Without you 'twould be broken.

Breslau, for September 29, 1907

Jesus' light

See how the birches
kiss in the light?
God's power enfolds them,
holds them tight.

Beloved, so we
are surrounded by light,
in joy and sorrow
together held tight.

Breslau, October 30, 1907

man Christian Student Union. In the letter that accompanied his poems of October 30, however, he wrote to Emmy, "Jesus has given me a wonderful victory since yesterday afternoon. I gave everything over to him and now trust him completely. He wants us to rejoice and give thanks when our opponents think we are full of pain and despair…I have made some verses about this, which you will receive." He sent the poems with a small print of two birch trees with crossed trunks.

Das Dunkel konnte weichen?
Wo ist die Finsternis?
Welch helles Himmelszeichen
durchbricht den Schattenriss?

Mein Herz war leer von Freude –
weithin kein Hoffnungsblick;
erfüllt mit schwerem Leide
schaut es auf Schmerz zurück.

Da zucken scharfe Strahlen
hinein ins wunde Herz.
Mir ist als hört' ich hallen:
Zur Sünde ward dein Schmerz.

Dein Leiden, das ist Sünde,
denn Jesus will es nicht.
Er ruft: O komm und finde
in mir dein Rettungslicht!

Da sank ich vor ihm nieder
und sagte meine Schuld.
Und er, er nahm mich wieder
in seine starke Huld.

Er selbst, der starke Jesus
durchbricht der Wolken Nacht.
Ihn haben, das ist Leben,
ihn sehen, Wundermacht.

Er will in allem Leide
erfreun mein Angesicht.

How could the gloom have yielded?
Where has the darkness fled?
From whence this heavenly brightness
among the shadows shed?

My heart was bare of gladness
and blinded by my plight –
weighed down by pain and suffering –
I saw no hope in sight,

until a harsh beam struck and lit
my wounded soul within –
and a voice spoke, telling me,
"Your grief is close to sin.

"Christ does not will that anguish
bind you to darkness grim.
He calls you to redemption –
to find your light in him."

'Twas then I bowed before him,
my shame and guilt to face,
and then that he received me
with the bounty of his grace.

'Tis Jesus, the strong Savior,
who breaks the clouds of night.
To find him is to live –
to see him, wondrous might.

In spite of every sorrow
he'll shine upon my face.

Wir sollen strahlen beide
in seiner Freude Licht!

So lass uns freudig sehen
auf ihn, den einz'gen Herrn!
Froh wolln wir vorwärts gehen,
sein Aug' bleibt unser Stern.

Breslau, 30. Oktober 1907

Halleluja, wenn die Freunde loben!
Halleluja, wenn die Feinde toben!
Halleluja, wenn in Not ich stehe!
Halleluja, wenn ich Hilfe sehe!
Halleluja, wenn die Sonne lacht!
Halleluja in Gewitternacht!
Halleluja in der Geistesfülle!
Halleluja in der Seele dürre!
Halleluja, wie es Gott auch wende!
Halleluja, stets und ohne Ende! Amen.

Breslau, 17. November 1907

In a long letter composed on November 17, Eberhard
writes, "This week was very hard. The main reason, I'm afraid,
was that several times I forgot about Jesus. Besides, my studies
were very difficult…and family matters very sad. The Student
Christian Movement crisis, the issue of baptism, the uncer-
tainty of my future – all this drained my courage and strength.

Both you and I shall radiate
the fullness of his grace.

And so let us together
on Jesus set our sights
and joyously go forward,
his eyes our guiding light.

Breslau, October 30, 1907

Hallelujah when friends offer praise!
Hallelujah when enemies rage!
Hallelujah when I suffer pain!
Hallelujah when help is on the way!
Hallelujah when the bright sun laughs!
Hallelujah in the storm's dark blast!
Hallelujah when my heart is bursting!
Hallelujah when my soul is thirsty!
Hallelujah, whate'er God deigns to send!
Hallelujah, forever, without end! Amen.

Breslau, November 17, 1907

So far, however, the Enemy has not been able to get me down,
because Jesus has protected me, and I keep taking refuge under
his cross! He remains my salvation, my sun, my shield. He is my
staff in the valley of gloom. And he will and must lead everything gloriously."

Ein Sehnsuchtsschrei!

O welche tiefe, heisse Glut
durchströmt mein wonnig frohes Herz!
Und doch, welch hohes Himmelsgut
zerreisst's zugleich im Sehnsuchtsschmerz?

O hört, o seht, o fasst es doch:
Es kann nur eine einz'ge sein!
Nach ihr das Blut pocht kochend hoch:
O wär', o wär' sie endlich mein!

O Amsel, Emmy, meine Braut!
Wie lange, lange bleibst du aus!
O hör's, so dich mein Blick nicht schaut,
bleibt tot und traurig jedes Haus!

O komm, o eil, o fliege doch!
O könnte ich nur hin zu dir!
O wäre es nur heute noch,
dass meine Einz'ge wär' bei mir!

Nur sehn, nur schauen will ich dich,
dein Aug', dein Haar und deinen Mund
ein einz'ges Mal will küssen ich!
Und ewig preis' ich diese Stund'!

O fühlte ich dein warmes Herz
entgegenschlagen meiner Brust!

On December 17 Eberhard wrote to Emmy, "I have just written a terribly stormy poem about you…" He sent it with an ac-

A cry of longing

How glorious the happiness
that burns and blazes in my heart!
And yet, how deep the heavenly pain
of longing that tears it apart!

Grasp my meaning: hear and see –
there is but one, and one alone
for whom my blood now pounds and seethes.
O what I'd give, were she my own!

O Emmy, sweetest songbird mine,
why must you linger far from here?
As long as I may not behold you,
every place seems dead and drear.

So hasten, come and fly to me
as I wish I could fly your way.
O would that my dear one were with me,
and would that she were here today!

One look is all I crave, that I
might see your eyes, your lips, your hair –
that I might kiss you even once.
I'd cherish such an hour fore'er.

Yes, could I only feel your heart
beat warm against my loving breast!

companying sketch: a cross rising from a rock at the edge of the
ocean, with waves dashing against it.

O löste sich der Sehnsucht Schmerz
in deiner Lieb' in lauter Lust!

Und Er?

Einer ist's, der drüber steht!
Er, der über alles geht!
Christ Kyrie! Ja, dir gehört die See!

Einer ist's, der Frieden gibt!
Er, der uns zuerst geliebt!
Christ Kyrie! Ja, dir gehorcht die See!

Breslau, 16. Dezember 1907

Amselchen!

Sahst du einmal eine Amsel
mit lieblich flinkem Flügelschlag
fröhlich singend hoch im Fluge?
Nahmst du wahr, wie sie die Freiheit
mit süsser Anmut zierlich krönt?
Ich, weisst du, kenn' nur eine Amsel!

Breslau, zum 25. Dezember 1907

Emmy's father often called her his Amselchen ("little black-bird") and Eberhard adopted the nickname.

O would love's agonies dissolve
and, through your love, become pure bliss!

And He?

There is one who stands above
all this, and rules our deepest love:
Christ, our Lord! Even the seas belong to thee.

He grants peace and stills our thirst,
and it is he who loved us first.
Christ, our Lord! Yes, the seas give ear to thee.

Breslau, December 16, 1907

Little blackbird

Have you ever watched a blackbird
nimbly beat her pretty wings,
or heard her sing with joy in flight?
Have you noticed how her freedom
is a crown of grace and charm?
I know, of course, but one such bird…

Breslau, for December 25, 1907

Hast du ein Amselpaar gesehen,
wie es sich schnäbelt flink und fein?
Ich weiss nur, wie so wunderschön
mein Amselchen küsst mich allein!

Dies Amselchen allein ich liebe
mit meiner ganzen Glut und Kraft.
Ja, ew'ge heil'ge Liebestriebe
mein Gott zu ihr ganz einzig schafft!

Und auch bei ihr ist alles Liebe.
Ich fühl' es ja in jedem Blick!
Die Welt viel eher ganz zerstiebe,
als dass verblasste dieses Glück!

Wie einzig sie ihr Köpfchen neigt!
Ja, Anmut krönt es stets aufs neu'!
Wie wonnig sie nur Liebreiz zeigt
in allem, sei es was es sei!

Oh, herrlich ist der Vögel Flug!
So frank und froh, so hoch und frei!
Es ist, als ob des Schöpfers Zug
nur ihm zum Lob die Triebkraft sei.

So froh und frei ist meine Amsel
zum Lobpreis seiner Herrlichkeit!
Ja, hoch empor steigt ihre Seele!
Ihr Herz macht Himmelswonne weit!

With the approach of the Christmas holidays, Herr von
Hollander relaxed his earlier injunction and allowed Eberhard
and Emmy to celebrate Christmas (and Emmy's birthday –

Have you ever seen how blackbirds
coo and bill and flit with glee?
How lucky, that my songbird
saves her kisses all for me!

There's no other that I cherish
with such depth; she makes me glow
with an endless, holy surge
of love by God on me bestowed.

Love fills my dearest dear as well,
I feel it in her every glance.
Sooner would fire consume the earth
than that our bliss should ever pass.

Yes, she exudes love's happiness,
and it crowns all she does with grace,
though most especially the way
in which she tilts her lovely face.

How glorious is the flight of birds –
so full of joy, so lithe and free,
as if God's hand were guiding them
to sing his praises endlessly.

My dearest one is just as happy,
God's praise is also her delight,
and as she spreads her joy to others
her soul climbs to heaven's height.

December 25) together. Ecstatic, Eberhard composed the
poem above, bound it with the one on the previous page, and
presented the little booklet as a gift.

So wie ein Vogel frei zu sein,
wie dort die Amsel auf dem Feld:
Ja, wahrer Freiheit Freudenschein
der Beste für das Höchste hält!

Die volle Freiheit kennet Amsel,
denn Jesus hat sie ganz befreit.
Kein Zwang sei je bei ihr zu finden,
denn Liebe füllt ihr Herz so weit!

Der Vögel Sang schallt hoch empor
von Amsel, Drossel, Fink und Star,
doch schöner als ihr schönster Chor
das Singen einer Amsel war!

Für Jesus! Hört, wie sie für Jesus
so fröhlich singt als Sonnenschein!
O seht, wie klar ihr Auge leuchtet,
für ihn ein Sonnenstrahl zu sein!

Mein Amselchen, das ist die Krone
der Schöpfung Gottes, unsres Herrn.
Ist sie in Jesus, seinem Sohne,
bleibt jeder Schatten von ihr fern!

Drum hoch mein Herz im Amselfluge,
mit freiem Schwung zu Gott empor!
Voll Glück erklinge jede Fuge
zu seiner Ehr' im höhern Chor!

Breslau, zum 25. Dezember 1907

Free as a bird on soaring wing –
like a blackbird over the field –
so is freedom and true joy:
the highest good the heart can yield.

My own blackbird knows this freedom,
for Jesus Christ has set her free.
May nothing stiff or formal spoil her.
Her heart is open for all to see.

Thrush and sparrow, starling, finch –
join the rising choir of sounds.
But lovelier than any choir,
my own sweet blackbird's voice resounds.

For Jesus! Hear her sing for him –
her cheerful notes rise through the air.
Her sparkling eyes reflect pure joy,
her praise rings out like sunlight clear.

My singing bird – she is the crown
of God's creation, near or far,
and while she lives and sings for Jesus,
no dark shadow can threaten her.

So up, my heart, on happy wings:
fly like a blackbird to God's throne.
Let joyous melodies resound
in praise of his high name alone!

Breslau, for December 25, 1907

Mein alles dir!

Wie mich verlanget,
ja, wie es mich zieht,
wie alles mich treibet,
das sagt dir kein Lied!

Das Herz – wie es pochet!
Das Blut – wie es rinnt!
Mein alles in Wallung
dir, Jesu sein Kind!

Dir zu den Füssen
mein alles sinkt hin,
in Liebe ersterbend
für dich Herz und Sinn!

Leben und Atmen,
mein Schaffen und Sein,
mein Geist und mein Körper,
mein alles ist dein!

So bin ich dein eigen,
auf ewig nur dein!
Doch dich gab ich Jesus.
So bleiben wir sein!

Breslau, 22. Januar 1908

After Christmas, Eberhard and Emmy were separated again and writing "only" two letters a week, as per her father's restrictions. In the one he sent with "All for you," Eberhard pleads, "Couldn't you write at least a few lines *every* day? That

All for you

How deeply I yearn for you,
how love compels
me and drives me and pulls me –
no song can tell.

My heart: how it pounds!
My blood runs wild.
My whole being pulses
for you, God's child.

I'd perish for love –
I'd fall right at your feet.
I love you with each breath
I take, each heart beat.

My life, breath, and being,
my work, and still more –
my body and spirit –
all are yours.

Yes, I am eternally
yours. Only this:
I gave you to Jesus,
and so we are his.

Breslau, January 22, 1908

would give me a better idea of how you are and what you are
doing. Of course, I don't mean you should send mail more than
twice a week."

Pest und Heil

Der Sünde Pesthauch steigt empor
und hüllt die Seele ein.
Du dünkst dich hinter Schloss und Tor,
und doch schleicht sie herein.

Durch Fugen schmal und ohne Licht
dringt ein der Sünde Hauch.
Du ahnst und merkst es lange nicht,
berauscht vom Höllenrauch.

Und tiefer, immer tiefer wird
dein Herz der Sünde Raub.
Vergebens mahnt und ruft der Hirt;
dein scharfes Ohr wird taub.

Der Bann liegt schwer und ernst auf dir!
Wo will mein Herz nur hin?
Und endlich dünkt dir's selber schier
als wär der Teufel drin.

O Seele, raff dich eilend auf,
der Herr, der Herr ist da!
O komm, o komm, im Fluge lauf,
denk, was am Kreuz geschah!

Ja, Sünde über Sünde ist
in deinem armen Sinn;
drum hast du nimmer keine Frist.
O leg, o leg sie hin!

Am Kreuzesfuss auf Golgatha
ist Platz für jedes Herz!

Sickness and healing

You thought yourself secure and safe,
and yet it still crept slowly in,
enveloping your very soul:
the pestilential fog of sin.

Through cracks too thin to let in light
its hellish fumes seeped bit by bit,
and thus it overwhelmed you
before you even noticed it.

Deeper and deeper you sank down –
your heavy heart, the prey of sin.
In vain, the shepherd's warning cry –
your ear, once sharp, was deaf to him.

Where will your helpless heart turn now?
The spell that holds you in its clasp
has brought your captive soul so low,
you're sure you're in the devil's grasp.

But there's still time to rouse yourself,
the Lord himself is on your side.
Come, run to him on eager feet,
and think how on the cross he died.

Yes, sin on sin has weighed you down
and crushed your weak and weary will,
but there's no end to Jesus' grace,
and he'll accept your burdens still.

At Golgotha, beneath the cross,
there's hope for every desperate soul.

Für dich ist er am Kreuze da,
er sühnt der Sünde Schmerz.

Hier ist kein Pesthauch, ist kein Grau'n,
hier ist nur Licht und Heil!
Drum musst du Jesum selber schaun,
auf ewig bei ihm weil'!

Ja, Jesu, tausendmal gelobt
seist du, nur du allein!
Und wenn der Böse noch so tobt,
am Kreuz, da bleib ich dein!

Breslau, 31. Januar 1908

Ganz für Jesus
sei mein Leben!
Ganz für Jesus
sei mein Sein!
Ihm, dem König
alles geben
bringt das Glück
ins Herz hinein!

Breslau, 8. April 1908

At the beginning of the letter he sent with "For Jesus alone!"
Eberhard writes to Emmy, "From this poem you can see that I
am very happy…happy because I am allowed to belong to Jesus
through a new purification. It is so important to find, again and
again, the points where a new surrender [to God] is necessary.

It is for *you* that he hangs there,
to heal you is his only goal.

Here are no horrors, here no plagues,
only salvation, only light.
So look to Christ himself and stay
eternally within his sight.

I praise thee, Lord, a thousand times,
yes, none but thee alone!
For at the cross, though Satan rage,
I will forever be your own.

Breslau, January 31, 1908

For Jesus alone!
So may I live
with all I have
and nothing less.
I'll give him all,
my Lord and King –
so will my heart
find happiness.

Breslau, April 8, 1908

Otherwise the Enemy will easily succeed…Everything, really
everything, depends on our belonging to the Lord so completely that the last remnant of self and the least trace of evil is
overcome for good."

Drum vorwärts, aufwärts! Schnell vergessen
sei alles, was gehemmt!

Voran mit Jesus! Tief gereinigt
stets treuer sei gekämpft!

Breslau, 12. April 1908

Ein Jahr dein eigen!

Ein Jahr ist nun vergangen,
ein Jahr so inhaltsschwer,
seit du mein Herz gefangen,
dass es dein eigen wär!

Es war ein Jahr der Gnade,
voll Kampf, voll Lust und Leid.
Sein Weg ging schmal und grade
empor zur Ewigkeit!

Es war die Nacht der Wonne
vor einem Jahr im Wald –
und heute scheint die Sonne,
das Glück ward mein so bald!

Wie tief ich damals flehte,
wie hoch mein Sehnen ging,
als Nachtwind mich umwehte
und Mondschein mich umfing.

Eberhard wrote this poem to mark the first anniversary of
their engagement. In the accompanying letter (April 15) he
writes: "Preparing for exams has kept me from prayer…and

Then forward, upward! and forget
all that held you back, unfree.

Onward with Jesus, deeply cleansed,
always more faithfully!

Breslau, April 12, 1908

Yours one year

Twelve most eventful months have passed –
one whole year come and gone –
since you, my dearest, stole my heart,
since I became your own.

It was a year of grace as well –
of struggle, pleasure, pain –
of following life's narrow path,
eternity to gain.

It opened with such rapture
on the heath, beneath the moon.
Today the sun is shining –
love's bliss was mine so soon!

How deep, how high, my hopes and pleas!
How earnestly I prayed,
while moonbeams bathed me with their light
and night winds round me played.

from writing poems. But yesterday I couldn't resist any longer –
I just had to write the enclosed lines. I then went out into the
park, in bright moonlight, to pray and to praise God."

Es war noch viel zu wenig,
was ich erschaut, erfleht;
es gab mein Herr und König
weit über mein Gebet.

So lieblich und so wonnig,
wie Emmy wirklich ist,
so strahlend, glücklich, sonnig
erträumt man's keiner Frist.

Das, was sie mir gegeben,
die süsse einz'ge Braut,
das hätte all mein Streben,
das kühnste, nicht erschaut.

Nein, tausendmal Millionen
hat sie mir mehr gebracht,
als aller Erden Zonen
sich hoffnungsfroh erdacht.

Sie hat mir mehr gegeben,
als alle Menschen sind –
sie gab mir ja ihr Leben!
Und Grössres niemand find't!

O Emmy, lass mich lieben
dich ganz mit tiefer Glut!
Lass mich mit allen Trieben,
mit jedem Tropfen Blut

nur dein für ewig bleiben,
ja, dein als ganzer Mann.
Von dir mich wegzutreiben
vermag nicht Tod noch Bann.

My vision then was far too small,
too little did I dare.
Yet God gave me a hundred times
what I begged him in prayer.

And now, see with what happiness
my dearest Emmy beams!
Of such bright radiance and joy
most hearts can only dream.

The gift that she, my dearest,
allowed me to receive,
I could not, in my boldest hours,
ever have conceived.

For she increased my joy
at least a millionfold; yes, more
than one could ever hope for here
or on earth's farthest shore.

Yes, she has given me more
than any other under heaven:
she gave her life to me entire,
and more cannot be given.

O Emmy! Let my love for you
wash o'er you as a flood,
that every passionate impulse,
my every drop of blood

be yours alone entirely,
yours always to abide.
No force of exile, threat of death
could drive me from your side.

In ew'ger Glut dir dienen,
von ganzem Herzen dein,
nur immer selig sinnen
was Glück dir könnte sein.

So ganz will ich dir leben,
du wonnig schöne Braut!
Es hat das höchste Streben
was Schönres nie erschaut.

Breslau, 14. April 1908

Der Weg ist licht und grade,
es geht um Gottes Sach'.
Wir folgen Jesus nach
mit neuer Bundeslade.

Der neue Bund ist Friede,
weil Gott in Christus sprach.
Wir folgen Jesus nach
mit freiem, frohem Liede.

Ob Sonnenschein seit immer
auf unserm Wege lag,
wir folgen Jesus nach.
Wir lassen Jesus nimmer.

The summer and fall of 1908 were tumultuous for both
Eberhard and Emmy. Else's baptism on August 2 was still making
waves in the household, Emmy was unwell, and there was no end
of strife between the young couple and their parents. On September 22, Eberhard received word from the Silesian State
Council that, because of his obstinacy with regard to baptism, he
would not be permitted to take his doctoral examinations in

May I, to serve you all our days,
my burning love employ,
and never tire to devise
whatever brings you joy.

So let my life be wholly yours,
my sunshine and my bride!
Let any search: no fairer love
on earth will e'er be spied.

Breslau, April 14, 1908

The path lies straight and shining:
our cause is the call of God!
We follow Jesus onward,
our bond with him renewing.

The Son of God is bringing
his peace, as promised long.
We follow Jesus onward
with cheerful, hopeful singing.

And should our path forever
be sunlit till the end –
we follow Jesus onward,
forsaking Jesus never.

theology. The next day, in an all-out family quarrel, Emmy's father accused Eberhard of being "unreliable and morally dubious," and attempted to cancel the young couple's engagement. Emmy dug in her heels and was turned out of the house (she found refuge with friends in Berlin). Eberhard left of his own accord; it would be more than a year before he entered the von Hollander residence again. Eberhard was baptized on October 25, 1908, and

Und geht's durch Not und Leiden,
durch Kreuzestod und Schmach,
wir folgen Jesus nach,
von ihm mag nichts uns scheiden.

Und wenn auch manche Lücke
der grosse Mörder brach,
wir folgen Jesus nach
auf blutgetränkter Brücke.

Die Nacht ist bald vergangen,
es naht der grosse Tag!
Wir folgen Jesus nach,
bis wir ans Ziel gelangen.

Eberhard & Emmy, 24.–25. September 1908

An meine Einzige!

Wir brauchen es uns nie zu sagen,
wir wissen es auch ohne Wort:
Von Liebe, Liebe stets getragen
gehören wir uns fort und fort!

Ja Liebe! Welch ein selig' Leben!
Ja Liebe! Welch ein Sonnenschein!
Wir brauchen nicht nach ihr zu streben,
sie strahlt von selbst ins Herz hinein.

was subsequently disowned by his parents. Emmy was baptized on December 22. In the spring of 1909 he moved to Erlangen and began working toward a doctorate in philosophy. Re: "The path lies straight and shining," Emmy wrote four of the verses in Halle on September 24; Eberhard added several more the next day, in Breslau. He reworked it into this version in 1935. A few

Come need and suffering ever,
or death, or bitter shame,
we follow Jesus onward –
no power can us sever.

And though the Murderer's wrath
has broken many a breach,
we follow Jesus onward,
a blood-drenched bridge our path.

Night will soon be defeated –
the great day is drawing nigh!
We'll follow Jesus onward
until our goal is completed.

Eberhard & Emmy, 24–25 September, 1908

To my only love

We know it without even speaking,
nor is there any need to say
that it is love alone that binds us.
Together we belong for aye.

Love is the happiness of living –
love is the radiance of the sun.
We need not seek it, for it freely flows,
into our hearts unbidden runs.

days after Eberhard's death, Emmy showed Marianne Zimmermann her collection of Eberhard's poems, and this one jumped out at her. "It was *the* word for the hour," Marianne remembered in 2001. "A tune came to me; I took a pen and wrote it down on the spot. I never altered it."

In Liebe schlagen unsre Herzen.
In Liebe sind wir völlig eins.
Die Liebe süsst uns alle Schmerzen.
In Liebe ist mein Leben deins!

Breslau, 28. September 1908

Die Rosen!

Die Rosen anzusehen
so lieblich und so süss
lässt sinnend viel erstehen:
Sie sagen das und dies.

Wie flüsternd sie sich neigen,
wie traulich dicht ihr Grün,
als wollten sie mir zeigen,
was stets mir steht im Sinn.

Aus dichtem Wald von Blättern,
als sei's dein wonnig' Haar,
so schlank die Blüten klettern
und bieten Grüsse dar!

Von deiner Lieb gebunden,
von dir als Gruss gesandt!
Oh, noch vor wenig' Stunden
da hielt sie deine Hand!

Du hast sie auserwählet
und hast an mich gedacht.

After Emmy sent him a bouquet of roses, Eberhard wrote,
"How shall I thank you! I believe this poem will tell you more

In love our hearts shall beat together.
In love we are forever one.
Through love, all pain is sweetened for us.
Through love, my life becomes your own.

Breslau, September 28, 1908

Roses

So beautiful and fragrant that
no other flower could compete,
these roses fill my mind with thoughts
of you – so distant, yet so sweet.

Whispering, they nod together,
friendly foliage entwined,
as if they intend to mirror
what is foremost in my mind.

Rising up from leafy bower,
offering their greeting fair,
slender, clambering, budding sprays –
enchanting as your hair.

Bound together by your love,
sent by you as greeting fond –
and it was only hours ago
that you held them in your hand.

You chose each one with me in mind,
a token of our love, I know,

than a letter could. It seems as if my love for you were growing
ever deeper, nobler, happier, and more trusting…"

Oh, was dich da beseelet,
hat mir der Strauss gesagt:

Rot ist die Farbe unsrer Liebe,
purpurrot dein süsser Mund.
Rot rollen auch der Adern Triebe,
mein Blut für dich zu jeder Stund'!

Und wie die süsse, zarte Knospe
so frei erhebt ihr wonnig' Haupt,
so unberührt ist meine Emmy.
Kein Sturm ihr je die Knospe raubt.

Und wie das rosa Blatt sich öffnet,
als breitet's seine Flügel hin,
so steht ihr Herz dem meinen offen,
erschliesst sich mir ihr Kindersinn.

Und wie die dritte Rose pranget,
so purpurrot, so sammetweich,
von jener Pracht sie nichts erlanget,
an der mein Amselchen so reich.

Doch wie so strahlend schön und dunkel
die Blätter ineinander stehn,
so denke ich an ein Gefunkel,
dagegen ist nichts andres schön!

Ich denke an zwei süsse Sterne,
so frisch, so lieb, so blau und klar.
Und ach, wie sah ich stets so gerne,
wenn dort auch eine Perle war!

Wie süss, wenn Amsel eine Träne
um mich als um ihr Liebchen weint,

and what was beating in your heart
these flowers tell me now:

One rose is red, and red your lips.
Red is true love's very hue.
Red is the blood that in me throbs
through every single vein for you.

Another, a sweet and tender bud
freely unfolding to perfect flower,
is untouched, like my own dear love –
a rose no wind or rain can mar.

Its delicate petals draw apart,
like wings outspreading, wide and free,
and like this blossom, she bares her heart,
reveals her childlike soul to me.

This rose, here, is smooth as satin,
in deep-hued crimson richly dressed,
but even it could never match
the fairness with which you are blest.

And while its clustered petals gleam
in dusky, jeweled splendor rare,
I see, above, another brightness
whose radiance is beyond compare.

I'm thinking of two stars I know,
sky-blue, lively, loving, clear:
your eyes, and brimming from them both
a shining pearl – a glistening tear.

How sweet, when my own darling weeps
o'er me, her best beloved, a tear,

wenn ich ihr Köpfchen an mich lehne,
und zarte Liebe uns vereint!

Und nun die volle, grosse Blüte!
O darf ich sagen, was sie meint?
Ja, wahrlich, Gottes Liebesgüte
als Sonne strahlend uns bescheint.

O glaube mir, geliebte Emmy!
Die Stunde ist uns nicht mehr fern,
wo du als meine Herzenssonne
stets bei mir bleibst als Lebensstern!

Breslau, 29. September 1908

Immergrün

Wie im Wald in tiefem Frieden
diese Blüten lieblich stehn,
so wird drüben wie hinieden
Jesu Glück nie von uns gehn!

Weil in Jesus wir gegründet,
weil in Gott wir selig sind,
drum die Liebe niemals schwindet,
„Immergrün" heisst „treu gesinnt".

Welches Glück und welche Wonne!
Ich bin dein, du ewig mein!
Welch ein Leben voller Sonne!
„Immergrün" heisst „glücklich sein".

Erlangen, 15. Mai 1909

On May 15, Eberhard wrote to Emmy from Erlangen, where
he was writing his dissertation on Nietzsche, "This morning I

and I press her head close to mine –
though far apart, in love we're near.

There's one more rose that far excels
all other flowers, for its gleam
reflects the light of God's great love,
which shines on us with radiant beam.

Take my word, dear Emmy!
The hour's no longer far away
when you, my heart's own sun and star,
forever at my side shall stay.

Breslau, September 29, 1908

Always green

As these lovely flowers growing
in a peaceful forest glade,
so the joy that comes from Jesus
to our hearts shall never fade.

Since it firmly rests on Jesus
and on God, who blesses us,
our love is like the periwinkle:
always green, for faithfulness.

I am yours, you're mine forever –
what delight, what endless bliss!
What a sun-filled life is ours –
as this flower of happiness!

Erlangen, May 15, 1909

got up at five o'clock and went for a wonderful hike to the
Atzelsberg, where I picked a bouquet of periwinkles for you."

Freiwillige vor! Ach, die Not ist's, die ruft,
das grosse, weltweite Verderben!
Zu Tausenden wanken sie friedlos zur Gruft,
Verzweiflung umnachtet ihr Sterben!

Freiwillige vor! In den Kampf, in den Streit!
Die Fahne des Kreuzes, sie winket!
Glückselig, wer Jesu sein Leben geweiht,
die Krone des Lebens ihm blinket!

15. Juli 1909

Sag mir, wer in diesen Jahren
die Liebe gab in unser Herz,
durch den es Gnadenjahre waren
in aller Freude, allem Schmerz!

Fragst du, wer für alle Lasten
die Kraft zum Tragen täglich gibt,
wer schenkt dem Herzen sel'ges Rasten?
Der sich für uns zu Tod' geliebt!

Fragst du, wer in unsrer Liebe
die Sonne aller Freude ist,
wer segnet unsrer Herzen Triebe?
Es ist der Heiland, Jesus Christ!

Es ist der Herr, der uns geleitet!
Es ist der Herr, der mit uns geht!

29. März 1917

Dedicated to "my best beloved little blackbird, on the tenth anniversary of our engagement," Eberhard wrote the poem "Tell me" in the Harz Mountains, where he and Emmy were on

Freewillingly forward! Give ear to the cry
of distress and world-wide corruption.
See how, by the thousands, men perish and die,
despairing and doomed to destruction.

Freewillingly forward! Into the strife
'neath our banner – the cross, of the Savior.
Happy is he who gives Jesus his life.
Christ's crown will be his forever.

July 15, 1909

Tell me who bestowed on us
the gift of love through all these years,
who o'ershadowed them all with grace
in joyous times, and times of tears.

Ask who it is, who gives us strength
to carry on, gives life and breath;
who is the heart's true resting place –
'tis he who loved us unto death.

Ask who it is, who is the sun
of our love's joy, whose radiance pours
its blessings on our hearts' desire –
it is our Savior, Christ the Lord.

It is the Lord who stands beside us!
He goes with us wherever we go!

March 29, 1917

a rare vacation, taking stock of the previous decade and seeking
clarity about their goals for the future.

Strahl, erlöse! Licht, befreie!
Durchleuchte alles bis zum Kern!
König Jesus, alles weihe,
du Sonnenaufgang, Morgenstern!

Deinem Leuchten wir vertrauen.
Du rufst aus Finsternissen auf.
Du wirst Strahlenwelten bauen
aus leuchtend reiner Feuertauf'!

Strahlenpfeiler hehrem Hause
erbaust du weit ins Land hinaus.
Brause, Flammengeist, erbrause!
Die Feuerflammen sende aus!

Heil'ge Weihe, nah uns, heile!
In Reinheit nur kann Leben sein.
Heil'ger Geist, verbleibe, weile!
Dein Zeichen ist der weisse Stein.

Sannerz, 1921

Wir glauben Unsichtbarem.
Wir glauben letztem Grund.
Wir glauben Offenbarem.
Wir glauben Stund um Stund.

Wir glauben stillem Funkeln.
Wir glauben innerm Wort.

The last line of "Light redeem!" refers to Revelation 2:17,
"To him who is victorious I will give the hidden manna; I will

Light, redeem! O save and free us.
Let thy beams pierce us to the core.
Consecrate all things, King Jesus,
thou rising sun, thou morning star.

Lord, we fully trust thy radiance.
Thy summons calls us out of night.
Brilliant light-worlds dost thou build
of fires baptismal, pure and bright.

Built on shining, radiant pillars,
thy sacred temple soon will stand.
Roar, O spirit of fire, roar loudly –
send out thy flames across the land!

Holy power, draw near and heal us:
alone in pureness can life shine.
Leave us not, O Holy Spirit –
a pure white stone thy sacred sign.

Sannerz, 1921

We believe the unseen being.
We believe the final power.
We believe what is revealed.
We believe hour by hour.

We believe the quiet glimmer.
We believe the inner word.

give him also a white stone, and on the stone will be written a
new name, known to none but him that receives it."

Wir glauben fest im Dunkeln.
Wir glauben hier wie dort.

Wir glauben Jesu Worten.
Wir glauben Geist und Kraft.
Tut auf euch, Lebenspforten,
der Glaube Neues schafft!

Sannerz, 1921

Unseren Kindern

Wie schwirrt es aus, das Volk der Bienen!
Welch grosses, grosses Einigsein!
Wie will es schaffen, will es dienen!
Hier gibt es niemals „mein" noch „dein".

Der Schwarm fliegt heim zum Kinderhüten.
Das Bienenvolk ist völlig eins!
Und was es sucht aus allen Blüten,
allein für sich lebt niemals eins!

Die Bienen kennen Einheitstriebe,
ein Wundergleichnis der Gemein!
Sie schaffen wie ein Volk der Liebe –
und niemand, niemand bleibt allein!

Sannerz, 1921

Written for a children's songbook, this poem reflects
Eberhard's lifelong fascination with the natural world, and his
insistence that nature study be part of every child's education,

We believe, although in darkness.
We believe here on earth.

We believe the words of Jesus.
We believe the Spirit's might.
Faith brings forth a new creation.
Open wide, O gates of life!

Sannerz, 1921

For our children

See how the bee-people swarm together –
what perfect oneness they display!
They build and serve and work as one.
With "mine" and "thine" they do away.

When they return to nurse their young,
then, too, they are completely one.
They share the harvest of each blossom,
and none lives for himself alone.

Bees know the impulse of true oneness –
a wondrous sign of community.
A people of love, they toil as one,
and none is left out of their unity.

Sannerz, 1921

so that each might grasp "the coherence of nature and of
mankind, and the unity and communal character of all forms
of life."

Sannerzer Weihnacht

Weihenacht! Du Nacht der Nächte,
die den Reichsten arm gemacht –
du durchleuchtest alle Mächte
und erhellst die dunkle Nacht.

Jesus ist der Sterne Leuchte.
Jesus ist des Lebens Kraft!
Was der Welt unmöglich deuchte,
Jesus allen Armen schafft.

Mach uns arm, wie du geworden,
Jesus, durch die Liebe arm!
Mach uns schwach in deiner Stärke –
unsrer Nöte dich erbarm!

Sannerz, 1921

Das Wort uns neu geöffnet
strahlt Wahrheit auf uns aus.
Wir schauen staunend, betend
des Geistes neues Haus.

Der Wahrheit neu geöffnet
hör'n lauschend wir den Ruf:
Er ruft, wie er's stets wollte,
hinauf – von Stuf' zu Stuf'!

Sein Weg ist neu geöffnet.
Das Reich ist jetzt uns nah.
Zur Macht wird seine Sendung:
Der Stärkere ist da!

Sannerz, ca. 1921

Sannerz Christmas

Christmas! Holy night of nights
that made the very Richest poor –
you pierce the darkness with your light;
powers of night cannot endure.

Jesus is the light of stars.
Jesus is the strength of life!
And he does for the world's poor,
things beyond the world's belief.

Make us poor through your great love,
Jesus, poor like you, we plead.
Make us weak – weak in your strength.
Show us mercy in our need.

Sannerz, 1921

Newly revealed, the Word
shines out its truth on us
as we view with prayerful awe
the Spirit's new-built house.

Newly wakened to the truth,
we listen to God's call,
as step by step he leads us
on the way he longs for all.

Newly opened, the way ahead
to the kingdom of God is clear.
His mission takes on power –
the Mighty One is here.

Sannerz, ca. 1921

Der Wille ist Kraft,
der Wille im Geist,
der alles erschafft,
das Wollen dich heisst.

Bereitschaft will Gott.
Sein Wille ist da.
Das Wollen tut not.
Das Nein will zum Ja.

Wo nirgends mehr Rat,
wo kaum ein Gefühl,
der Glaube wird Tat.
Der Wille hat Ziel.

Das Alte wird Nacht,
wenn Glaube erglüht.
Der Wille erwacht.
Der Funke ersprüht.

Der Eigensinn stirbt.
Das Dürre vergeht.
Wenn Gott um uns wirbt,
der Glaube ersteht.

Der Glaube trat ein.
Der Umschwung ward wahr.
Der Wille allein
ist wirkend und klar.

Over 2,500 visitors inundated Sannerz in 1921, and many of them sought Eberhard's advice. Counseling the confused, encouraging the weary, and diffusing interpersonal tensions, he

The will is a power.
In the spirit, it calls
you forth and gives
shape and form to all.

God's will is plain:
he seeks readiness –
so let your will answer.
Let your no become yes.

When all feeling is gone
and all counsel fails,
then faith becomes action –
a goal fills its sails.

Night swallows what's old
when faith catches fire.
The will reawakes,
sparks leap ever higher.

What's withered burns up
and self-will dies.
Whom God claims as his,
in him faith will arise.

Faith's entered in –
true conversion is here.
Now the will is pure
and active and clear.

must have worn himself to the bone at times. But as this poem
indicates, he never doubted that life's deepest questions could
be answered by every person who truly sought God's will.

Der Wille ist Gott,
der Liebe dir gibt.
Wo alles war tot,
wird Leben, das liebt.

Sannerz, ca. 1921

Wir glauben dir. Die Tat erwache,
die Tat des Glaubens, der dir glaubt!
Die Glaubenswahrheit deiner Sache
ergreife Herz und Hand und Haupt!

Die Liebe tut es, was du wolltest.
Du wolltest stets, wir wollten nicht.
Du wolltest jeden, dem du grolltest.
Wir widerstrebten dem Gericht.

Wir wollten dich in unsern Herzen.
Wir wollten fühlen, wie du fühlst.
Wir lieben dich in Todesschmerzen.
Wir sagen Ja, worauf du zielst.

Wir wollen leben dir, du Wille.
Wir wollen tun, was du uns sagst.
In dir wird alles Eigne stille.
Wir tuen nichts, was du nicht magst.

Was du erforderst, willst du geben!
Was du verheissen, wirkst du ganz!
Dein Wille ist die Kraft zum Leben,
die Liebe deiner Sonne Glanz.

Sannerz, ca. 1921

God is this will,
and he gives from above
new life, where all
was dead, and new love.

Sannerz, ca. 1921

We believe. May deeds now follow,
deeds that faith in you demands.
May the truth of your great vision
grip us, heart and head and hand.

Love accomplishes your will.
We rebel; your will remains.
You chasten everyone you seek,
yet we resist your judgment's pain.

Deep in our hearts we long for you.
We love you in death's sore distress.
We yearn to feel just as you feel.
Where'er you lead, we will say yes.

We want to live for you alone.
We want to do as you direct –
in you, our selfish will to silence,
whatever grieves you to reject.

What you require of us, you give!
All that you promise, you fulfill!
The radiance of your sun is love,
and strength to live, your holy will.

Sannerz, ca. 1921

EBERHARD ARNOLD

Nun ist es wahr:
Der Herr ist mein!
Herrscher der Schar,
nun bin ich dein!

Herrscher des Lichts:
Du bist's allein.
Ich bin ein Nichts,
lebend als dein!

Sannerz, 1921–22

In Fesseln der Not
in Fesseln der Lust
in Fesseln des Trugs
in Fesseln des Kriegs.

In Ketten die Welt
es hält sie das Geld
bedeckt sie mit Kot
in Fesseln der Not.

In Ketten der Leib
erniedrigt das Weib
verwickelt in Wust
in Fesseln der Lust.

In Ketten das Werk
erstickt in dem Berg

Eberhard's frequent public speaking tours took him to
Munich, Dresden, Frankfurt, Berlin, and other large cities,
where he found a "great longing for something new," but also
the "unmistakable bondage to evil" that he describes in the

'Tis true at last:
the Lord is mine.
Ruler of all,
I am now thine.

The Lord of light
art thou alone.
I am nothing –
my life is thy own.

Sannerz, 1921–22

In fetters of need,
in fetters of lust,
in fetters of fraud,
in fetters of war.

The world is in chains,
enslaved by greed
and covered in muck –
in fetters of need.

Bodies are shackled,
and women are thrust
into bondage – entangled
in fetters of lust.

Under mountains of lies
our work is stalled –

poem, "In fetters of need." Note, in the last verse, an allusion to
the resentment that millions of Germans felt over their
"shameful" defeat in 1918, and over the humiliating war com-
pensations demanded by the Allies.

des lastenden Trugs
in Fesseln des Lugs.

In Ketten der Kampf
im modernden Krampf
verlorenen Siegs
in Fesseln des Kriegs.

Fleestedt, 1921 oder 1922

Kräfte schwinden – Mächte stürzen!
Die Zeit zerbricht!
Augen blinden. Jahre kürzen
das Welt-Gericht!

Massen sterben. Menschen enden.
Der Tag ist aus.
Erd-Verderben! Welten-Wenden!
Letzter Graus!

Mauern sinken. Türme schwanken.
Gewalt vergeht.
Sterne blinken, Herzen danken.
Das Reich ersteht!

Gottes Kommen! Christi Nahen!
Die Gotteszeit
wird vernommen! Seher sahen
die Wirklichkeit!

Sannerz, 1922

1922 began with growing tensions at Sannerz. By summer,
things came to a head, and some forty members abandoned the
household. Devastating as this crisis was, Eberhard refused to

by the weight of deceit,
by the fetters of fraud.

The battle is stalled
in the grudges of yore,
in decay and defeat –
in the fetters of war.

Fleestedt, 1921 or 1922

Powers collapse, strength drains away.
Time breaks down.
Sight fails, the years race quickly by.
World judgment sounds.

Masses die, whole peoples perish.
Day is gone.
Earth's ravaged, worlds are overturned.
The horror's come.

Towers rock, walls crumble, fall.
Brute force subsides.
Stars appear, and hearts give thanks.
The kingdom's nigh!

God's approach, Christ's coming,
the age divine – now here –
is tangible as seers saw it:
as reality.

Sannerz, 1922

engage in mud-slinging or concede defeat. He chose instead to
use the exodus as a chance to re-found the community on its
original center, Christ.

EBERHARD ARNOLD

Du, du! Jesus-Geist, was auch geschah,
ich traue dir.

Du, du, auferweckt, bist immer da,
ich sehe dich.

Du, du! Was bin ich? Wie ich auch war,
ich glaube dir!

Du, du, Weltenkraft, reichst Leben dar,
ich geb' mich dir.

Du, du, siehst auch den, der dich verriet,
ich liebe dich.

Du, du, Kommender! Dein Reich geschieht,
ich warte dein.

Sannerz, 1922

Dass Friede werde –
Gottes Reich die Erde
ganz besitze;
dass alle Herzen
frei von Hasses Schmerzen
Brüder werden:
Der Bund beschwöre,
Freund wie Gegner höre
diese Losung:

Written after the painful Sannerz crisis, "Thou, thou"
was set to music two years later by Alexander Weichert, an old
family friend. Eberhard's son Heini regarded it as one of his

Thou, thou spirit of Christ,
whatever has been, I trust in thee.

Thou, thou risen one,
art ever here: I see thee.

Thou, thou! What am I?
Whatever I've been, I rest in thee!

Thou, thou power of the world,
thou givest life: I give thee mine.

Thou, thou rememberest those
who turned on thee. I love thee.

Thou, thou coming one:
thy kingdom comes. I wait for thee.

Sannerz, 1922

May peace awaken,
and earth be overtaken
by God's kingdom.
And may all aching hearts
freed from hatred's dread smart,
yet become brothers.
Hear me, both friend or foe,
I implore you to know
and heed this watchword:

father's deepest poems and said that, along with "Jesus: thou,"
which Weichert also set to music (p. 209) it should not be over-
used, but sung "only at holy moments."

In Christus Reinheit –
das ist unsrer Einheit
Bund und Freundschaft.

Sannerz, 1922

Dem Sonnenaufgang entgegen

Dämmrung flutet, Hoffnung schwindet,
Tempel brechen. Nichts mehr bindet.
Der Tag vergeht.

Schwarze Gifte, rote Gluten,
Lichter nebeln, gelbes Wuten,
der Abend gärt.

Schwangre Wolken, schwüle Hitze,
dunkle Mächte schleudern Blitze.
Die Nacht erwacht.

Trunknes Taumeln, Leidenschaften,
Ketten! Peitschen! Stieres Haften.
Die Nacht ist schwer.

Düstres Ringen! Wüste Kämpfe!
Herzzerbrechen! Gliederkrämpfe!
Die Not ist da!

Hohler Tand, groteske Leere,
Neid und Zank und gift'ge Schwere.
Die Schlange herrscht.

How Eberhard weathered the 1922 crisis on a personal level might best be guessed from this poem, according to his biographer, Markus Baum: "Eberhard was no superhero. The

in Jesus' purity,
there is our friendship
and our unity.

Sannerz, 1922

Toward the sunrise

Twilight falls, hope flees the heart.
Temples collapse, things fall apart
as day departs.

Poisons black, embers red,
yellow rage – lights mist and fade:
dusk's brewing shade.

Sultry, brooding storm clouds break.
Dark powers hurl forked lightning, shake
the night awake.

Passions, staggering drunkenness.
Chains, whips, stubborn mindlessness.
Night's heavy breath.

Gloomy struggles, fights unrestrained.
Broken hearts, limbs cramped, constrained –
no end of pain.

Vacant glitter, void grotesque.
Strife, envy, toxic heaviness –
the Snake's bequest.

breakup of his community sapped his strength…For months,
he fought attacks of self-doubt and depression. In his poem 'Toward the sunrise' he describes the quarreling, poison, strife, and

Missverstehen! Gift'ge Dämpfe!
Sprachverwirrung! Bruderkämpfe!
Der Geist verfinstert!

Harte Menschen, bittre Nöte
stossen aufwärts steil Gebete.
Der Morgen naht.

Durch das Dunkel dämmert Hoffen.
Ferner Strahl hat uns getroffen:
der Morgenstern!

Überm Chaos glitzern Lichter,
und das Licht erlöst als Richter.
Die Sonne glüht!

Alles schwindet, was geblendet.
Was gefesselt, endlich endet.
Der Aufgang kommt!

Ruder schlagen, Wellen glänzen!
Augen lachen, Blumen kränzen.
Die Sonne strahlt!

Friede lächelt. Freude reinigt.
Geist erlöst. Die Wahrheit einigt.
Der Tag ist da!

Gifte weichen, Ketten fallen.
Freiheit bindet. Jubel hallen:
Der Herr regiert!

Sannerz, Frühling 1923

envy he experienced. But in the eighth verse, he unexpectedly
announces, 'Morning nears.' It is a symbolic sunrise: truth
breaks in; love is victorious. And by the poem's end, he is stat-

Misunderstandings, venoms stirred.
Quarreling brothers, confusion of words –
minds are blurred.

Hardened souls and bitter fears,
prayers sent upward with fierce tears.
Morning nears.

Now hope glimmers through the dark.
A faint beam meets us from afar:
the morning star,

while o'er the chaos of the night,
burns with judging, saving light
the sunshine bright.

Illusions lift and disappear –
gone at last all bonds, all fear:
dawn breaks here.

Oars swing in rhythm, ripples gleam.
'Neath flower garlands, faces beam
as sunlight streams.

Peace smiles, and before our eyes,
truth unites, joy purifies:
God's day draws nigh.

Poisons yield like falling chains.
Joy abounds, free and unfeigned.
The Lord now reigns.

Sannerz, spring 1923

ing emphatically, 'The Lord now reigns.' It was this certainty
that kept him from falling into self-destructive brooding – a
rock-like certainty that always won the day."

Schweigende Andacht!
Durch den Wald
klingt leise Zwitschern,
kein Ruf hallt.

Wir warten lauschend,
horchend auf,
Winde leis rauschend –
kleiner Hauf.

Er will nun sprechen.
Wir sind still.
Alles soll brechen,
wie er's will.

Geist – er soll bauen
heiligen Dom.
Lasst ihm uns trauen,
flutendem Strom.

Frei von dem Alten,
stark in Dir.
Du nur sollst walten
jetzt und hier.

Waltende Freiheit!
Aufwärts reisst
ewige Neuheit,
heil'ger Geist!

Benneckenstein, April 1923

Eberhard wrote this poem at a youth conference in the
Harz Mountains. Regarding its theme, Emmy writes in her
memoirs, "All of us sensed that, hidden in nature, lay a mystery.
Many had never experienced God or had lost sight of him

Silent devotions.
From treetops tall
soft twitters resound,
but not one call.

We wait, listen –
a tiny band.
Soft winds murmur
all around.

Let God speak now.
Let us be still.
All else must shatter
as he wills.

The Spirit shall build
a holy dwelling.
Trust in his great
stream upwelling.

In thee we're strong,
freed from old ways.
Thou alone rulest
here, today.

The Holy Spirit
reigns here free –
awakens, renews
eternally.

Benneckenstein, April 1923

through disillusionment with the established churches…Out in
nature, however, people sensed something…of the unknown
God, and had great reverence for him."

Ich fange wieder an zu leben.
Die Nacht entweicht, der Tod versinkt.
Der Leib will seine Glieder heben,
der Frühling rauscht. DieSonne winkt.

Refrain:
    Wer greift den Blitz? Wer hält die Sonne?
    Der Blitz entzündet. Die Sonne glüht.
    Durchschauert sein in Ahnungswonne
    ist sel'ges Warten dem, der sieht.

Ich fange wieder an zu glauben.
Der Mut steht auf, der Geist erwacht.
Ich schreite wie durch Rosenlauben.
Das Leben dehnt sich, steigt und dacht.

Ich fange wieder an zu lieben.
Des Frühlings Farbenduft geht um.
Die Todeskälte ist zerstieben,
die liebesleere Nacht herum.

Sannerz, Mai 1923

In Stille versunken,
zur Frühe ganz einsam,
so sammeln sich Funken
zur Freude gemeinsam.

Es öffnen sich Herzen,
es schliessen sich Kreise,

Written the first spring after the Sannerz crisis, "I have begun to live again" reflects Eberhard's new joy after what must
have been one of the hardest winters of his life. Walther
Böhme, a friend, set it to music in 1924.

I have begun to live again.
The night retreats, death sinks away.
My body stirs, my limbs awake.
Spring breezes whisper, sunbeams play.

Refrain:
Who grasps the lightning in his hand?
Who holds the sun and makes it blaze?
To see is to tremble in awe and bliss
and know hope's blessings all your days.

I've started to believe again.
My courage rises, my spirit revives.
I walk as if through rose-filled arbors.
Life spreads and stretches, upward strives.

And I've begun to love again.
Spring's fragrance wafts upon the air.
Death's coldness is at last dispersed,
the loveless night chased to its lair.

Sannerz, May 1923

Out of the silence,
alone in the dawn,
bright sparks come together,
in gladness now join.

Hearts are opened,
and circles closed.

From Emmy's memoirs: "Early morning meetings at Sannerz had a deep meaning for us… Anyone who was at peace with God and his brothers and sisters could take part; those who were not stayed away. At six o'clock we gathered around the

es finden sich Menschen
erneuerter Weise.

Es schwingen sich Glieder,
es reichen sich Hände,
es klingen die Lieder,
dass alles sich wende.

Die Herzen sich finden
in heiliger Reinheit.
Die Kränze sich winden
in leuchtender Einheit.

Sannerz, Mai 1923

Das Tal liegt offen da,
die Sonne flutet drüber hin.
Geöffnet sei die Seele dir,
geöffnet, aufgetan,
dass ich dir hingegossen bin,
dir stille halte, jetzt und hier.

Die Augen auf für dich!
Im Riesenschöpfungsüberblick
muss ich ins Weite schaun, ins Tal:
Ja, du bist gross! nicht ich.
In dir bist du, kein Einzelstück,
in deinem All gibts keine Wahl.

kitchen fire…in silence, listening, a powerful spirit of expectation
living in us. It seemed the kingdom could break in any day! After

Men find one another:
a new wind blows.

Dancing and swaying,
hands join the round.
All life is renewed –
glad music resounds.

Heart meets heart
with purity crowned.
In unity radiant
garlands are bound.

Sannerz, May 1923

The valley opens wide,
and sunshine floods it full of light.
O may my soul awake to thee,
to thee be opened wide –
that I for thee may be outpoured
and wait in stillness for thy word.

My eyes, be lifted high
to view creation's wondrous might,
to gaze far out across the land –
yea, thou art great! not I.
Thou, only one, art all in all.
In thee there is no other call.

this we went to work – in the office, in the garden, in the
children's room, and elsewhere around the house."

Das Oder-Weder fort!
Im Ew'gen gilt's im All zu sein.
Die Strahlen weiten ewig sich,
sind weder hier noch dort,
sind überall – der Raum ist dein!
Ich glaube dir, ich gebe mich.

Weit, weit, unendlich weit
geht Gottes Geist, wie unser Land.
Er lebt in allem, was nur lebt,
weht über Felder breit,
ist über Wälder ausgespannt.
Er treibt, wo Leben ist und webt.

Die weite Landschaft hier
ist uns Symbol des Friedensreichs.
Das Grün und Blau ist Farbe uns:
Wir lieben Hoffnung,wir,
wir wollen Bläue tiefen Teichs,
wir suchen Treue dir, nur dir!

Gott: du bist gross, so gross!
Das weite Land ist dir nur klein.
Wir lieben ohne Ufer dich,
dein Geist ist grenzenlos.
Ganz ohne Schranken sind wir dein.
In dir bist du, kein Einzel-Ich.

Sannerz, Mai 1923

Set to music by Alexander Weichert the same year it was
written, "The valley opens wide" was often sung at Sannerz and
(later) the Rhön Bruderhof. Marianne Zimmermann writes: "I

No other choice is mine.
Eternity rules in the spheres.
Its radiance forever streams,
and it is not confined,
but everywhere. All space is thine –
and so I give thee all that's mine.

As boundless and as wide
as is this land, so is our God.
His spirit plays across the fields;
in all that lives, he hides.
He hovers o'er the woodland trees –
a moving, pulsing, living breeze.

This wide and lovely scene's
a symbol of God's reign of peace.
Its colors are our colors –
for our hope is always green,
and with the depth of waters blue,
we would be loyal to thee, and true.

God, thou art without end!
To thee the widest land is small.
Thy spirit knows no bounds;
so, too, we love thee without end.
Yes, we are wholly, fully thine:
none stands apart, in space or time.

Sannerz, May 1923

will never forget those meetings on the Küppel – the hill behind our house – with the vast countryside lying open before
us. The view certainly helped broaden our inner horizon."

EBERHARD ARNOLD | 201

Es öffnen sich Himmel,
es strömt aus den Schleusen.
Der Winde Getümmel
die Tore aufreissen.

Es öffnen sich Pforten,
es weiten sich Türen.
Erblickst du es dorten?
Der Geist will dich führen!

Es öffnen sich Hütten.
Die stets sich versagen
beginnen zu bitten,
weit auf, es zu wagen!

Es öffnen sich Herzen.
Es schliessen sich Kreise.
Es finden sich Menschen
in heiliger Weise.

Sannerz, Mai 1923

Gott bewegt

Ich vergeh', tiefer wächst die Not.
Gott sucht Schuld. Er versinkt in Tod.
Das Opfer Gottes stirbt hinein:
In blut'ger Schmach macht Tod uns rein.

In a letter to a close friend, Eberhard writes (January 30, 1923) "Now is the moment to reclaim the truth everywhere! In speech, in song, and through the printed word, above all in work and life…one message must be spread near and far:

The heavens are opening
like floodgates – it pours.
The turmoil of tempests
has torn down the doors.

Now gates are unlocking
and opening wide.
Do you see it? Believe:
the Spirit will guide.

In the humblest homes,
where nobody cared,
at last men are open,
to pray, and to dare.

As hearts are opened,
new circles are bound.
Souls find one another
on holy ground.

Sannerz, May 1923

God moves

I must cease. As need and suffering grow,
God takes on guilt, down into death must go,
for us becomes a sacrifice,
through blood and shame us purifies.

Jesus. Again and again, everything that people cling to must be
shattered…so that through dying, they may find resurrection…
renewed faith in Christ…courage for discipleship…and the
ever-new victory of the coming kingdom of God."

EBERHARD ARNOLD | **203**

Ich bin Tod. Gott wirkt, webt und schwebt!
Gott spannt Blitz. Dehnend, Schwungkraft lebt!
In Gottes Himmel Weltkraft schwingt
der Glut-Geschosse Reigen: Funken winkt.

Mensch baut Stein. Mauer fest soll sein.
Gott wogt, wächst ewiger als Stein.
Die Brunnen Gottes stürzen steil:
Gegossener Blitze Sause-Pfeil.

Ich bin Fluch. Dunkles steigt hinauf.
Gott macht frei, löst der Gifte Lauf.
Im Überstrom verfliesst der Schlamm.
In Reinheit strahlt der Wellenkamm.

Gott ist Kraft, dringt stets neu hervor.
Immer frei, Springquell schiesst empor!
Die Ströme Gottes sickern nie
im Rauschen ew'ger Melodie.

Springflut steigt. Aufwärts jagt der Strom.
Hochauf ragt Kristallendom:
bewegter Bau! Getürmt! Weit! Hoch!
In Wasserflut gefestigt doch.

Alles strömt, Fels zerspringt in Flut.
Alles rollt: Leib durchjagt das Blut.
Wenn Winde wehen, Schwüle weicht.
Wenn Sterne kreisen, Sonne steigt!

Heini Arnold once said, "When my father saw, in himself, something that hindered Christ, he brought it before the cross and fought it through… After such struggles he would often write a victorious poem…and when he came out of his study

I am death. God lives and moves and works.
His surging pow'r, tight strung, as lightning forks
and spans the skies in cosmic arcs
of dancing flames and glowing sparks.

Man builds with stone. His walls rise firm and tall.
Yet what God builds fore'er outlasts them all.
His springs plunge to the depths below
like liquid lightning from a bow.

I am a curse. Though powers of dark increase,
God acts, and when the poisonous slime, released,
runs off in a torrential stream,
the pure, clear waters crest and gleam.

God is strength. He wells up endlessly,
a fountain leaping upward, always free.
His rivers never will run dry,
nor will their music ever die.

The spring tide rises, drives the water higher,
and from it shoots a sparkling crystal spire.
Tossing, turrets spurt and spread –
swept downward and yet still upheld.

All is in flux: cliffs tumble toward the flood.
Through every coursing vein there races blood.
Winds blow, dispel the sultry air.
Stars orbit, now the sun is there!

he would be radiant – simply *radiant* with joy and love." Heini
was not referring to this specific poem, but he could have been,
given its opening – "I am death…I am a curse" – and its build-
up to a victorious ending where Christ "makes all new."

Gott bewegt. Nie ist er wie Stahl.
Gott ist Glut, Gott ist stets ein Strahl:
Er ist, wo Flammen lodern, glühn.
Er ist, wo Wasserquellen sprühn.

Gott ist Geist: Wehn, das stets bewegt.
Gott ist Kraft: Webend, was sich regt.
Gott bleibt als Liebe allem frei!
Christus erlöst, wirkt alles neu!

Sannerz, 1923

Rhythmisch schwingen sich die Glieder,
Herz zu Herz erklingt es wieder:
Die Reinheit lebt!

    Freuden-Funken,
    erst ganz einsam
    still versunken,
    bald gemeinsam
    in eins gewebt!

Solch Begegnen kann nicht schwinden,
wieder müssen wir uns finden.
Der Tag sich hebt!

Sannerz, 1923

From Emmy's memoirs: "We used to talk together until the early hours of the morning. Many times our discussions became quite heated, but we were usually able to end on a har-

God moves: he's not a steel-hard beam.
He is a fire: a steady, glowing gleam.
He is where flames leap, flare, and play.
He is where fountains burst in spray.

God is a spirit: an ever blowing breeze.
God is power: he quickens all that breathes.
His love is free to all, and true
in Christ, who saves, and makes all new.

Sannerz, 1923

In rhythmic joy we dance and swing,
and heart to heart, the echoes ring:
for pure love lives.

   Sparks of joy,
   at first alone
   and sunk in silence,
   soon unite
   and flare as one.

Such a gathering cannot end,
for we must find each other again.
Daylight reigns!

Sannerz, 1923

monious note. Often we would end with a quiet dance, moving in a circle as we sang."

Jesus: Du,
Reinheitsbad,
ew'ge Ruh',
Friedensstadt.

Wasch uns rein,
Stromes-Quell,
tauch uns ein
weiss und hell!

Ozean!
Lichtes-Meer!
Sternen-Bahn!
Wiederkehr!

Leucht uns rein:
Lichter-Bad,
Strahlen-Schein,
Sonnen-Rad!

Sannerz, 1923

Die Laterne in der Hand,
ziehen froh wir ein ins Land!
Den'n zur Rechten, den'n zur Linken
müssen allen Licht wir winken!
Auf durchs Land! Eins das Band!
Licht zur Hand!

Sannerz, 1923

At Sannerz the yearly lantern procession, a German tradition, gained new meaning: it symbolized the light of Christ being carried out into the darkness by his followers.

Jesus: thou
eternal balm,
cleansing bath,
city of calm.

Wash us clean,
rushing spring,
clear and bright –
plunge us in.

Ocean vast,
sea of heav'n,
path of stars,
turn home again.

Cleanse us
in thy bath of light,
wheeling sun,
radiance bright.

Sannerz, 1923

Lanterns swinging in our hands,
we walk singing through the land.
Turn to the left, turn to the right –
everyone must see the light!
Up through the land, as one band,
light in hand.

Sannerz, 1923

For something Heini said about the poem "Jesus, thou" see
page 188.

Gott ist Band.
Nehmt die Hand!
Gott ist Bund
jetzt zur Stund.

Schliesst den Kreis!
Bunt und weiss,
nehmt zum Tanz
Blumen-Kranz!

Geist-gepackt
schwingt im Takt,
Schritt zu Schritt,
Kreis zur Mitt'!

Sternen-Tanz!
Sonnen-Kranz!
Sphären-Klang!
Himmels-Sang!

Gott ist Klang,
Licht – Meer – Sang.
Lausch und sieh:
Harmonie!

Sannerz, 1923

Recalling the daily "inner gatherings" that took place in the
first years at Sannerz, Emmy writes in her memoirs that they
made her "shiver with a deep joy and thankfulness…Something
of eternity was living among us; something that made us forget
the limits of time and space…For those of us who experienced
those years, the 'first love' remains unforgettable…It is quite

God is our bond.
Take his hand.
Make your vow
unto him now.   .

Close the ring
with joy, and sing!
Dance in white
with garlands bright.

Spirit-primed,
move in time,
round and round,
center bound.

Starry dance
of suns, advance.
Music of spheres:
heaven to our ears!

God is the clang
of light, sea, and song.
Listen, see –
harmony!

Sannerz, 1923

clear, of course, that no one can live off memories of the past.
Today too the Spirit lives, calling people to 'Repent, for the
kingdom of heaven is at hand!' Yet for every person the time of
his first zeal and love will always be significant, and in times of
weakness he will be able to turn back to it, as to a reservoir of
strength."

EBERHARD ARNOLD | 211

Dein Geist ist wahr –
du sendest lautren Strahl.
Dein Licht ist klar –
du führst zum Einheitsmahl.

Dein Geist ist rein –
du löst der Welten Qual.
Du giesst den Wein –
du füllst der Sehnsucht Gral.

Dein Geist vereint,
gibt Macht zum Friedensreich.
Das Reich erscheint
in Kraft und Geist zugleich!

Sannerz, 1923

Gott ist Geist und Kraft,
Apostelgeist, Apostelkraft:
Mächte hingerafft!
Die Höllengeister weggeschafft.

Gott, du Kraft und Geist,
der Totes aus dem Abgrund reisst,
Geist des Christus heisst,
um Erd und Himmel ewig kreist.

Gott fegt Sand und Staub.
Er rüttelt Bäume, schüttelt Laub.

Speaking about the first years at Sannerz, Eberhard once
said, "The Holy Spirit brought us face to face with the presence
of God. Our rooms were filled with a power in those early days,

Thy spirit is true –
thy light gives purity.
Its clear ray leads
to the Meal of Unity.

Thy spirit is pure –
world's torment dost thou heal.
Thou pourest wine,
longing's grail dost thou fill.

Thy spirit unites –
gives strength for peace to reign.
In spirit and might
shall thy kingdom come again.

Sannerz, 1923

God is spirit and fire –
apostle might, apostle pow'r.
He breaks the force of evil spells
and sweeps away the ghosts of hell.

God, thou spirit and might
that tears the dead from abysmal night,
thou art the Christ,
forever circling earth and skies.

God drives dust and sand,
shakes leaves and trees across the land,

a power that did not originate from us who were living there,
nor from those who were our guests. It was a power from God
that visited us, an invisible power that surrounded us."

Spreu ist Windes-Raub.
Von ihm gefasst, dem Geiste glaub!

Geist der Reinheit: Gott!
Verweh, was faul und alt und tot!
Fülle unsre Not!
Verjag der Pest Verwesungs-Tod!

Geist beugt Feld und Wald,
als Sturm und Donner braust und hallt,
Wolken festgeballt,
wenn alles weithin tot und kalt.

Geist des Christus: Du!
Du wehest Tore auf und zu,
Sturmes-Stoss: im Nu
trägst du die ew'ge Kraft und Ruh.

Geist erfüllt, durchdringt;
Berg-Alpen-Mauern überspringt,
Fernsten Nähe bringt;
weit allen Windes-Frische bringt.

Sannerz, 1923

Kämpfender Heere Nachtmärsche verdringen,
der Tempel domt!
Drohender Mächte Gewalten verklingen:
der Friede kommt.

Set to music by Alexander Weichert, "The trampling"
made a deep impression on Marianne Zimmermann, who re-
called (2002), "When I first came to the Bruderhof in 1932, I was

blows the chaff in gusts –
the man he grips must trust.

Spirit of pureness – God! –
drive out what's rotten, dead, and old.
Calm our fear and pain,
chase off the plague of death's decay.

Field and wood he bends,
storm and echoing tumult sends,
and mighty thunderheads,
while all below is cold and dead.

Spirit of Christ, O Lord,
thy breath unlocks and closes doors
with rushing wind – but then
eternal calm and strength dost send.

God's spirit fills it all,
strides o'er the highest mountain wall,
and brings the farthest close –
yes, far and wide his fresh wind blows.

Sannerz, 1923

The trampling of night's warring armies
    grows fainter –
the temple-dome appears.
The threat and the tumult of battle fade
as peace draws near.

shaken by the forcefulness and fervor with which the community
sang this song, with its passionate words of confrontation and
battle – images of the spiritual fight."

Tobender Wellen Gebirge verbauschen,
der Sturm vergeht!
Reissender Wölfe Gegiere verrauschen:
der Geist ersteht.

Quälender Gluten Erregung verschwindet,
die Sucht erliegt.
Strahlenden Lichtes Reinheit verbindet:
die Freude siegt.

Biegender Schnörkel Verdrehung sich rundet,
der Lug hört auf.
Ragender Gradheit Emporkraft gesundet
der Wahrheit Lauf!

Sannerz, 1923

Grossstadt im Strudel!
Gepeitschtes Volk!
Jagende Rudel
in grauem Gewolk.

Menschen in Ferne
nahe gepresst.
Stadt ohne Sterne –
Gott dich verlässt.

Reflecting the hopelessness of the large cities he visited on
speaking tours, "The city: a maelstrom" captures a mood
Eberhard describes in a letter to a friend, January 20, 1923, "In
the hard struggle behind all these outward horrors that weigh
us down, one feels deep disillusionment and general depression
everywhere. There is a marked increase of the grimmest sort

The rage of the fierce, foaming billows is stilled –
the storm has passed.
The wrath of ravening war-wolves is tamed
by the Spirit at last.

Gone is the fever, the torment of passion –
gone lust's fell sway.
The pureness of radiant light now unites us:
joy rules the day.

Falsehood and scheming have fled
    with the darkness –
no lie remains.
Healing and lifting us, truth spreads its wings,
forever to reign.

Sannerz, 1923

The city: a maelstrom
of frenzied crowds.
Roaming hordes
beneath gray clouds.

Inhabitants distant,
though bodily pressed.
Streets without stars:
God has left.

of nationalism…Large circles of German youth are betraying
the sign of the Wandervögel with the swastika. Where are
those who…wear the sign of the Crucified One? There is a
great emptiness…What will fill this vacuum? Will it be the old
filth all over again, the old degenerate nature? Or will it be a
fresh, new wind of pure air – the holy breath of God?"

Liebes-Entseelung,
saugendes Meer,
Todes-Vermählung –
alles ist leer.

Langsames Sterben.
Schleichender Schluss.
Ödes Verderben.
Träger Genuss.

Ekel am Leben.
Glanz überall.
Blutiger Reben
berauschte Qual.

Gequälte Gesichter.
Schwülende Not.
Vertrübende Lichter.
Grossstadt ist Tod.

Lebens-Erneurung –
heute so fern!
Heilige Steurung,
greife den Kern!

Ihr Lüfte, erkrachet!
Stürme, erweht!
Propheten, erwachet!
Geister! ersteht!

Sannerz, ca. 1923–1924

Souls emptied of love,
a life-sucking sea.
Death-bringing marriages,
dull misery.

Slow-moving death,
creeping, then still.
Depravity, boredom,
another tired thrill.

Loathing for life,
despite all the glitter.
Bloody vines' drunken
torment bitter.

Twisted faces.
Oppression's breath.
Dimming lights.
The city is death.

If only renewal –
now so far away –
with holy force
could take hold today!

Let loose the tempest!
Atmospheres, break!
You prophets, arise!
Spirits, awake!

Sannerz, ca. 1923–1924

Mensch

Mensch! Du Herz, Leib, Geist und Seele!
Heilig deine Glieder stähle.
Harter Kampf steht dir bevor.
Gib dich ganz! Folg deinem Sehnen!
Lass den Blick sich unendlich dehnen!
Neig dem Allklang ganz dein Ohr!

Siehst du nun die Wogen steigen?
Lausch dem Klang der Todes-Reigen:
Letzte Not ringt schwer um Licht.
Totentanz auf dunklen Fluten!
Daseins-Kämpfende verbluten!
Liebeleeres Weltgericht?

Schau nur: Strahlen siehst du leuchten,
Tränen funkelnd Wangen feuchten:
Liebeleer ist letztlich nichts.
Daseinskampf schweigt vor dem Bruder!
Gegen-Hilfe hebt das Ruder:
Ehr auch du den Sieg des Lichts!

Fahr ins Meer, ins Todes-Leben!
Lass dich mit der Flut verweben.
Recke, spanne, schwinge dich!
Friedens-Kämpfer, Tod-Erleider!
Geist-Leib-Mensch! Du Seele beider!
Gib dem Lebens-Geist dein Ich!

Stuttgart, Februar 1924

Likely written with the Stuttgart YMCA in mind, Eberhard
wrote this while on a public speaking tour, one of several he

Man

Man – heart, body, soul, and spirit –
steel yourself, put on your armor:
mighty battles stand ahead.
Give yourself with every fiber,
lift your eyes to the horizon,
keep your ear tuned to the heavens.

Don't you see the breakers rising?
Don't you hear the death knell sounding
in the last hard fight for light?
This dance of death on dark'ning waves,
this bloody struggle to be saved,
is this world judgment's final hour?

Wait – the first faint beams are brightening,
tears on moistened cheeks are glistening.
Lovelessness is never the end.
Forget survival: find your brother.
Help each other take the rudder.
Praise the victory of light.

Steer out to sea, through death, to life!
Swim outward with the ebbing tide.
Stretch every limb, strain every nerve.
Man – heart, body, soul, and breath –
peace-fighter, sufferer of death –
give all for life: give your whole self!

Stuttgart, February 1924

made in 1924. Other destinations included Nordhausen, Leipzig, Chemnitz, and Dresden.

Alles schweigt.
Und wir ahnen,
wie tief in Äthernacht
Sterntag steigt.

Alles lauscht.
Und wir glauben,
dass aus der Todeswelt
Leben kommt.

Weltenweit
muss es leuchten.
In Raum und Zeit
erglüht Ewigkeit.

Jesus winkt.
Und wir staunen,
wie hell von weitem her
Leuchte blinkt.

Jesus naht.
Und wir schauen,
wie er, der zu uns kommt,
Sonne hat.

Jesus ruft.
Und wir hören.
Sein Rufen trägt uns zu
Geistes-Luft.

Jesus lebt!
Und wir leben,
und über Todesluft
Leben schwebt.

All is silent,
and we sense
how, deep beneath night's veil,
star-day breaks.

All things wait,
and we believe
that from the dying world
new life wakes.

In all worlds
the light must shine –
throughout all space and time
eternity gleams.

Jesus beckons,
and we marvel
how clearly from afar
his light beams.

Jesus nears,
and we watch
as he who comes to us
holds the sun.

Jesus calls,
and we hear
his voice – a spirit that
fills our lungs.

Jesus lives –
we live with him.
Life hovers over death's
atmosphere.

EBERHARD ARNOLD

Jesus siegt!
Leuchtend, schreitend!
Das Chaos – neu und eins –
unterliegt!

Sannerz, 26. Juli 1924

Der Schlern

Felsen schwören. Riffe rufen.
Steine schreien, dass es hören
alle Stufen aller Reihen.

Menschenkinder! Ihr verderbet
ohne Rettung. Ihr seid Sünder.
Ihr ersterbet in Verkettung.

Schwarzer Berge dunkle Schwere
bilden düster Felsensärge.
Geister-Heere leis' Geflüster

zerren Sünden alter Tagen
aus den Nebeln. Ohne Schwinden
Zacken ragen, wie mit Hebeln

hochgewuchtet – immer steiler –
in die Lüfte. Tief geschluchtet
in die Pfeiler sind die Klüfte.

A dramatic massif in the South Tirol, where Eberhard spent
eighteen months in 1913–1914, the Schlern is recognizable by
its huge "fingers" – enormous rock outcroppings that jut up-
wards for hundreds of feet and are visible for miles. Note the
complexity of the rhyme scheme. In each verse the third and

Jesus conquers,
radiant, striding.
He transforms chaos,
brings unity.

Sannerz, July 26, 1924

The Schlern

Cliffs are clamoring, rocks are roaring,
crags are crying, carrying echoes
from the heights down to the hollows –

sons of men! – while you lie, wasting,
stained by sin, without salvation,
perishing in chains and shackles.

'Neath heavy peaks, the gathering gloom
of crypt-like caverns and granite tombs
hides whispering hosts of spirit-ghosts

who strain the sins of bygone days
from out the mist. Now high peaks rear,
their summits clear – as if hoisted

by huge levers. Looming spires,
they rise still higher toward the skies –
great pillars over deep-cut chasms.

fourth syllables of the first line rhyme with the last two syllables of the second line; the third and fourth syllables of the
second line rhyme with the last two syllables of the third line;
and the third and fourth syllables of the third line rhyme with
the last two syllables of the first line.

Eingebettet im Gerölle
finstrer Gründe, angekettet
reckt die Hölle ihre Schlünde.

Harter Erde Felsen-Riffe
heben Finger, Schwur-Gebärde
aus der Tiefe, aus dem Zwinger.

Felsen schwören, Riffe rufen,
Steine schreien, dass es hören
alle Stufen aller Reihen.

Menschenkinder! Ihr verderbet
ohne Rettung! Ihr seid Sünder,
ihr ersterbet in Verkettung.

Doch über dunkeln Felsengraten
Sonne leuchtet! Rot erfunkeln
Strahlen-Saaten! Tau erfeuchtet.

Sonnenlichter – Himmelsgluten
hoch erstrahlen! Immer dichter
Feuerfluten Sonne malen!

Winde wehen. Atem webet
Äther-Reine. Auferstehen
lichtbelebet tote Steine.

Licht befeuchtet Gemsen, Rehe.
Felsenblösse ward erleuchtet.
Welche Höhe! Welche Grösse!

Menschen-Kleinheit! Herzerbebend
schau der Höhe Berges-Reinheit!
Neu erlebend Gott ich sehe.

Chained beneath them, where the raw
debris and rubble tumble, fall,
hell, though bound, throws wide its maw.

From the depths of this dark dungeon,
frozen earth uncurls her fingers,
swearing a defiant oath.

Cliffs are clamoring, rocks are roaring,
crags are crying, carrying echoes
from the heights down to the hollows –

sons of men! – while you lie, wasting,
stained by sin, without salvation,
perishing in chains and shackles.

But then: above the rocky ridge
the red and shimmering sun breaks through
like sunbeam-seeds on glistening dew.

Flames of sunlight, flares of heaven –
blaze up brighter, hotter, higher –
paint the sky with floods of fire.

Winds are blowing, moving, weaving,
with ethereal pureness breathing
new light into lifeless stones.

Over deer and chamois streaming,
sunlight falls, on sheer cliffs gleaming –
what grand heights, what majesty!

How small is man! With trembling heart
I see the high peaks' pureness, start
to live again, for I see God.

Steine: Bebet! Atmet, Wände!
Atem, wehe! Felsen, hebet
eure Hände auf zur Höhe!

Steine, lebet! Felsen, windet
Lebenskränze! Gräser, bebet!
Lichter, kündet neue Lenze!

Strahlen weben Frühlingsherrschaft.
Hört die Freude! Seht das Leben!
Gottes-Herrschaft nahet heute.

Sannerz, 1924

Auf zum Gefechte klar,
auf zu der Lichtes-Schar,
alle vereint!
Greift die Dämonen an,
brechet dem Lichte Bahn!
Gebt eure Freiheit dran,
Streiter zu sein!

Auf zu dem Strahlen-Sieg,
auf zu dem harten Krieg!
Werft euch hinein!
Krieger dem Mein und Dein,

Recalling the origin of the poem, "Up, join the battle now!"
Karl Keiderling, who joined Sannerz as a young man, said,
"One day Eberhard called me into his study: 'Come, sit down.
I've made a poem for your birthday. I want you to sing it for
me, so I can see if the words fit the melody.' The tune was an

You rocks and walls: heave, quake, and breathe!
You winds, spring up! You cliffs, lift up
your hands and raise them to the skies.

You rocks, awake to life, and flower.
Bind every crag with living bowers.
You grasses, nod! Lights, herald spring!

Bright beams are weaving spring's domain.
O hear and see! New joy holds sway:
God's kingdom has drawn near today.

Sannerz, 1924

Up, join the battle now!
Up, with the hosts of light,
united all.
Demons of darkness smite,
break through a path for light –
give all for truth and right,
fighters to be.

Up, for light's victory:
wage hard war constantly,
throw yourselves in!
Warriors against mine and thine,

old anarchist freedom song I had brought with me to the
community…I sang the song three or four times, while
Eberhard changed and improved it. From then on we sang it
with his new words."

Kämpfer dem Schlechten sein,
gebt euch zum Tode drein:
Streiter zu sein!

Auf zu dem Glaubens-Heil,
steigt auf die Gipfel steil,
klimmet hinauf!
Kehrt euch dem Abgrund ab,
kommt aus dem Massengrab
frei von dem Gut und Hab,
Streiter zu sein!

Sannerz, 25. März 1925

Du bist die erste Liebe,
du bist die gute Tat.
Du weckst des Geistes Triebe.
Dein Geist ist Kraft und Rat!

In dir, Marias Sohne,
lebt sanfter Mutter-Geist.
Die Güte ein uns wohne,
die zur Gemeinde weist!

In dir ist Kindesseele,
du bist der Kindergeist.
Das Kindesherz erwähle,
du, der du Menschkind heisst!

Du bist der einzig Reine,
du bist der wahre Leib,

combat all base design –
stand till death end your strife,
fighters to be.

Up, in faith's saving power!
Mount where steep summits tower –
upward aspire.
Turn from the dark abyss,
flee the mass grave of distress,
free and possessionless,
fighters to be.

Sannerz, March 25, 1925

You are the impulse of first love,
the root of each good deed.
Your spirit wakes and strengthens us,
us counsels in our need.

In you, O Son of Mary,
dwells the spirit of the mother.
May it dwell within us, too,
and lead us to our brothers.

You are the childlike spirit,
the soul of each true child.
Choose the simple-hearted,
O child of man so mild.

You are the only pure one,
your body is true alone.

belebest Menschen-Steine,
machst einig Mann und Weib.

Du bist die Mannes-Seele,
du bist die starke Kraft.
Entfache, glüh und stähle!
Gib Glut, in eins gerafft!

Zur Einheit wird der Glaube,
der wartend dich geliebt.
Du hebst uns auf vom Staube,
du, der die Schuld vergibt.

Du liebest deine Feinde,
das ist dein Mannesmut.
Dein Geist bewirkt Gemeinde.
Du liebst in Mutterglut.

Du bist der einzig Eine.
In dir ist alles eins.
Das Meine bleibt das Deine.
Was Feind war, wird jetzt deins.

Sannerz, 1925

Durch Todesnot zu fahren
in dunkler Schicksalshaft,
zu fahren mit den Scharen
zerbrochner Sterbe-Kraft,

On New Year's Eve 1925, the date of "Through deadly peril,"
Eberhard baptized his son Heini, Karl Keiderling, and Lotte
Henze. Taking place at the *Waldquelle,* a spring near Sannerz, the

You join man to woman
and quicken hearts of stone.

You are the truest soul of man:
you are his strength, his might.
Set us afire, and temper us –
unite us in your light.

Where faithful hearts await you
in love, grows unity.
You raise us from the dust,
forgive our sins, us free.

You love your bitterest enemies
with manly courage firm.
Your spirit brings community –
motherly and warm.

You are the one and only:
in you, all things are one.
What's mine is yours forever –
by you all foes are won.

Sannerz, 1925

Through deadly peril sailing,
driven by a sinister fate,
go throngs whose strength is failing,
a broken, dying freight –

baptism marked the culmination of a long and difficult spiritual
battle not only for Lotte, who had been possessed by demons,
but for the whole household at Sannerz.

verzweifelt – ohne Gnade –
in Finsternis verdammt,
ist rettungsloser Schade.
Die Freifahrt ist verrammt.

Da winkt vom andern Ufer
ein Lichtes-Augen-Stern.
Es winkt der Ufer-Rufer
und trifft im Herz den Kern.

Der Ruf weckt totes Leben,
bewegt Geburten-Grund.
Erstorbne Glieder heben
sich auf zum Lebens-Bund.

Erheben sich die Scharen
heraus aus Todesqual,
erneut zum Licht zu fahren,
so schliesst sich ihre Zahl.

Jetzt ward der Bund geeinigt,
der Ring ist rund und fest.
Es ward die Hand gereinigt,
die nun den Ring nicht lässt.

Neu ruft der Ruf die Scharen,
der Ruf zur Todesfahrt,
lebend zum Tod zu fahren,
zum Leben nun bewahrt.

Der Mut ergreift die Scharen,
zur Todesnacht hinab,
zur Hölle hinzufahren,
zu siegen selbst im Grab.

despairing, without mercy
condemned, a foundering wreck
whose way ahead by darkness
impenetrable is blocked.

But wait: a light is beckoning,
a shining eye from shore.
And now a voice is calling,
it strikes the heart's deep core.

It rouses, wakes the dying,
and stirs the inmost womb.
Now withered limbs are rising
to bond with life anew.

And as they rise and stand again,
from death's dark pangs released,
the throngs sail on toward the light,
their close-bound ranks increased.

Renewed, they are united –
a circle firm, secure,
each hand the circle grasping,
by loyalty made pure.

The voice calls out once more –
this time a cry that takes their breath:
"Sail right on into death, alive,
and thus be saved from death."

But courage arms their hearts anew
to sail on through the waves
toward death's night – to hell itself,
to conquer o'er the grave.

Der Tod wirkt neues Leben,
denn Gott bricht Grab und Sarg.
Der Fels muss sich erheben,
die Schwächsten werden stark.

Die tot, erstorben waren,
die brechen Weg und Bahn.
Der Ruf beseelt die Scharen,
sie tragen ihn voran.

Sannerz, Jahreswende 1925–26

Finstrer Nebel! Wolken-Schwärze!
Erde! Dunkler Stern!
Unkraut! Laster! Mörder-Herze!
Bleibt das Licht dir fern?

Volks-Versammlung – Lärm-Getümmel –
Pauken, Blech-Musik.
Hinten schrillen arme Lümmel,
Mädels: Störungs-Trick.

Unbeirrtes Vorwärtsdringen!
Buntes Farbenbild!
Machtgefülltes Liedersingen
trifft das Strassen-Wild.

Wort wird Kraft, Gewalt, Dynamik,
Blitze funkeln hell,

Though Eberhard wrote "Gloomy mists," with its vivid
description of a public meeting (a Nazi rally?) seven years before Hitler took power, he had been concerned about the

From death, new life arises,
for God destroys at length
death's vaults; removes the boulder,
and gives the weakest strength.

The once-dead throngs now gather
and rise to blaze the trail.
God's call enlivens them; it leads
them onward without fail.

Sannerz, New Year's Eve 1925

Gloomy mists, lowering clouds –
earth, darkened star.
Rank weeds, vice – murderous hearts!
Is it a wonder the light is far?

A rally: turmoil, commotion, noise –
pounding drums and blaring brass.
At the back, coy girls distract;
hoodlums heckle, stare.

Nothing can stop the forward march,
the colorful display!
Rousing songs hit every street,
join the echoing fray.

Words unleash dynamic powers;
lightning-like they flash,

growing influence of the so-called Brown Shirts since 1921,
when they had taken over the Bavarian branch of the German
Worker's Party.

EBERHARD ARNOLD

ohne Sprechkunst und Keramik,
kunstlos, schlagend, grell.

Energien, kraftgeschwängert,
bringen Macht und Licht.
Kurz wird nur die Frist verlängert:
Rettung und Gericht!

Über aller Ungewitter
Höllen-Leidenschaft,
über alle Teufels-Ritter
triumphiert die Kraft.

Wem gehört die Macht der Erde,
wem die Welt-Gewalt?
Welche Vollmacht spricht: „Es werde!",
strahlt, wenn Donner hallt?

Gott ist Kraft, ist Macht im Tode.
Gott ist's dem, der glaubt.
Grabe! Pflüge! Egge! Rode!
Unkraut Gott beraubt.

Stern wird frei. Denn Gott ist mächtig.
Unkraut fliegt hinweg.
Geist wird freudig, strahlend, prächtig.
Christus bahnt den Steg.

Laster sind hinweggestossen,
Teufels-Mächte fort.
Kleine Menschen sind im grossen
weiten Hafen-Port.

devoid of form or eloquence –
artless, harsh, crass.

Forceful energies of light
impregnated with power
herald judgment, redemption –
portend the final hour.

Far above the storms and tempests,
above the devil's bands –
above the raging hellish passions
another Power stands.

Who is it who rules the earth?
Who made the universe?
At whose command does life spring,
lightning flash, clouds burst?

This force is God, if you believe,
even at death's hour –
so till your heart, root out each weed
that robs him of his power.

Earth shall be free, for God is might,
he sweeps all evil away.
The Spirit of radiant joy shall come,
and Christ shall lead the way.

Vice and wickedness are banished,
Satan's might destroyed.
God brings us little men into
his harbor safe and wide.

Sicherung ist jetzt gewonnen,
Angriffslust ersteht.
Feindeskräfte sind zerronnen,
Sieges-Atem weht.

Christus einigt allvergebend,
Jesus führt voran.
Christus füllt uns allbelebend,
er ist Weg und Bahn.

Vorwärts denn mit Christi Kräften!
Auf ins Feindesland!
Starken Strom in reinen Säften
bündet heil'ges Band.

Sannerz, Februar 1926

Das Leben ist Not,
es bringt uns den Tod:
im Sterben Verderben,
in Trümmern die Scherben.

Das Leben ist Wehr,
ein Kämpfen so schwer:
Verwundete stärken
in wirkenden Werken.

Das Leben ist Sieg
im härtesten Krieg,
kann Tote erwecken
zu Kämpen und Recken.

Protected and secure at last
they burn to storm the foe –
enemy forces scattering
as winds of victory blow.

Christ unites them, all-forgiving –
he is their guiding staff.
He enlivens and revives them,
is himself their path.

Onward, then, in Jesus' strength,
into the hostile land!
His blood – our one pure impulse –
unites our holy band.

Sannerz, February 1926

To live is to suffer,
for death is life's end –
dying, decaying,
shattered and spent.

To live is to fight –
to resist till you bleed,
and then bind up the wounded,
strong in your deeds.

To live is to triumph
in the fiercest of fights,
rousing the lifeless
as warriors in strife.

Das Leben – es glaubt,
ob alles geraubt,
sagt Kampf an den Mächten,
ergibt sich dem Rechten.

Das Leben im Geist
dem Sarge entreisst.
Aus Beelzebubs Rachen
Erstorbne erwachen!

Sannerz, Karwoche 1926

Strahle herab!
Sonne der ewigen Liebe,
dass alle feindlichen Triebe
sinken ins Grab!

Feuer verzehrt!
Alles dem Tode Geweihtes,
alle Gewalten des Neides,
Feuer verzehrt!

Leuchtet empor!
Sonnen der glühenden Strahlen,
Sterne unzählbarer Zahlen,
leuchtet empor!

Brechet herein!
Kräfte der ewigen Gluten,
Ströme der lodernden Fluten,
Weihe zu sein!

"Radiance, descend!" was signed by Eberhard and Emmy.

To live is to trust,
though robbed of all things,
to cry war on dark pow'rs,
yield alone to the King.

Life in the Spirit!
Snatched from their graves,
from Beelzebub's jaws,
the dead awake, saved.

Sannerz, Holy Week 1926

Radiance, descend!
Thou sun of all love eternal,
every impulse infernal
to the grave send.

Fire, burn away
all things to death consecrated,
all that with envy is weighted.
Consume it today.

Blaze forth with light,
suns of bright, brilliant beams,
stars in countless burning streams –
flare up with might!

Break in, we plead,
powers of eternal radiance glowing,
flood of fiery love o'erflowing,
hallowed to thee!

Strahle herauf!
Du auferstandenes Leben,
ewige Kräfte zu geben,
strahle herauf!

Sannerz, Ostern 1926

Die Flammenaugen brennen,
sie glühn die Schlacken aus.
Die Feuerblicke kennen
den Stahl, das Gold heraus.

Durchglühtes Gold muss blitzen.
Gebrannter Stahl ist fest.
Des Geistes Schläge sitzen.
Die Glut nur Reinheit lässt.

Der Stahl wird sichre Waffe.
Das Gold erstrahlt im Licht.
Der Geist den Mann erstraffe.
Das Edle dunkle nicht.

Das reine Gold im Herzen,
voran zur heissen Schlacht!
Erhebet hoch die Kerzen
der Fackeln Feuermacht.

Sannerz, 26. Juli 1926

Eberhard loved the symbolism of fire; he wrote this poem on his forty-third birthday and presented it to Emmy.

Shatter our night,
thou, who from death truly arose,
from whom pow'r everlasting flows.
Send forth thy light!

Sannerz, Easter 1926

By flaming tongues of fire
the dross is burned away,
their red-hot eyes discerning
the iron and gold – that stays.

Gold, once refined, will glitter,
and iron hardens to steel.
The Spirit's blows strike squarely –
pure metal they reveal.

Steel makes a trusty weapon,
and gold gleams in the light.
So may the Spirit temper us
and keep what's precious bright.

With hearts made pure, then, forward!
Take up the hardest fight.
Raise high your flaming torches
and send afar their light.

Sannerz, July 26, 1926

EBERHARD ARNOLD

245

Wehender Stimm-Hall!
Sehnendes Zittern!
Einsam im Welt-All
ohne Erwidern!

Ahnend' Erinnern
todwunder Herzen,
Zwiefach im Innern
Aufschrei der Schmerzen.

Leidende Süchte
ziehen zur Erde,
stehen im Lichte:
Freiheit! Entwerde!

Freiendes Retten
sinkender Masten!
Lösung der Ketten
bleierner Lasten!

Freiheit ist Stärke
sieghafter Kräfte,
strahlend im Werke
strömender Säfte.

Lodernde Sonne
fliehender Nächte!
Freudige Wonne
liebender Mächte!

Stehend vom Falle
lodernder Kerne.

Eberhard gave this poem to his sister-in-law Else von Hollander on her birthday, December 13, 1926, with the following

Drifting, trembling,
aching voice –
alone in the universe
echoless.

Foreboding remembrance –
wounded hearts' pain –
outburst of anguished
souls rent in twain.

Driven by obsessions,
dragged to the ground –
brought into the light:
freed! unbound!

Rescue, save
the foundering ship.
Chains, be loosed –
leaden weights, slip.

Freedom: strength
of victorious forces –
streaming sap
of creative sources.

Blazing sun
that ends dark hours –
joyous bliss
of loving powers.

Up from the deep,
from the central fire,

dedication: "Full unity comes to us when God's love, his love to all his creatures, fills our hearts and rules our lives."

EBERHARD ARNOLD

Einheit im Alle
steigender Sterne.

Liebende Wesen,
strahlende Augen –
totkrank genesen!
Schau, wie sie taugen!

Liebe zu allen,
Einheit im Einen,
ihm zu gefallen,
Treue im Reinen.

Sannerz, Dezember 1926

Wir sehen uns wieder
in Kampf oder Ruh.
Es strahlt zu uns nieder
der Lichtblitz im Nu.

Wir sehen uns wieder
in Heimat zu Haus'!
Wir sehen uns wieder
im Kampfes-Gebraus.

Wir sehen uns wieder
in Liebe ganz eins.
Wir sehen uns wieder,
es fehlt uns dann keins.

Wir sehen uns wieder
bei Licht oder Nacht.

in cosmic union,
stars rise higher.

Loving souls
with radiant eyes –
once deathly ill,
now worthy and wise.

Love toward all,
oneness in One –
steadfast and pure,
for his sake alone.

Sannerz, December 1926

We'll meet once again
in struggle or calm,
lit up by a sudden flash
on us come down.

We'll meet once again
at home, as of old.
We'll meet once again
where battles unfold.

We'll meet once again
as one, at all costs,
united in love –
and none shall be lost.

We'll meet once again
by night or by day.

Wir sehen uns wieder,
wenn alles erwacht!

1926–1927 (?)

I. Der Tod

Die düster finstre Nacht
von ewigem Gewicht
hat uns den Tod gebracht.
Ihr Sterben ist Gericht.

Des Teufels Fluch-Gewalt,
des Todes Schwert-Gewaff
hat Sünden-Macht geballt
in Wolken fest und straff.

II. Ewige Gewalt

Ewiges Gericht
der dunklen Zornes-Macht.
Bleiernes Gewicht,
du hast den Tod gebracht.

Der Tod ist uns verhasst.
Erstaunend, wartend, leis,
stumm den Sarg umfasst,
so standen wir im Kreis.

Rhönbruderhof, Jahreswende 1927–1928

These two poems were written after the death of Ursula
Keiderling, a baby, on December 30, 1927.

We'll meet once again
when all reawakes.

1926–1927 (?)

I. Death

The gloominess of night –
an oppressive, endless weight –
has brought us death itself,
and judged us with her fate.

Satan's power accurséd –
the leveling sword of death –
has pierced the compact thunderclouds
of sin, and taken our breath.

II. Eternal force

Judgment eternal
of anger's dark breath,
leaden weight infernal:
you have brought us death.

Surrounding the casket,
loathing death's hand,
dismayed, yet expectant,
silent we stand.

Rhön Bruderhof, New Year's Eve 1927

In Heilung und Weihe, so nehmet den Geist;
in kämpfender Reihe dem Dunkel entreisst.
Was doppelt in Zweiheit, vereinigt in eins.
Die Einheit in Dreiheit verstösst euer keins.

Es ist nun geschehen – der Geist, er ist da.
Dämonen verwehen, das Reich ist uns nah.
Die Dunkel entweichen, die Nächte entfliehn.
Bei göttlichen Zeichen die Teufel verziehn.

Du Gottesmensch stehe und gehe in Tod.
Gemeindegeist wehe, führ Du unser Boot.
Es wagen die Scharen, von Stürmen geweht,
ins Dunkel zu fahren, die Segel gebläht.

Die Hände du lege Entzweiten aufs Haupt.
Die Herzen bewege, dem Dunkel entraubt.
Die Flammen erlodern, der Rauch steigt empor.
Die Trümmer vermodern, die Fackel dringt vor!

Rhönbruderhof, Anfang 1928

Wir sind so schlecht und niedrig,
verscheuchen oft den Geist,
wenn heiliges Sturmesbrausen
die kleine Schar umkreist.

Wir trotzen bös und widrig
dem heiligen guten Geist,

In 1926, the Sannerzers bought the Sparhof, a rundown
farmstead, and a few families moved there to begin renovations.
In September 1927 the last members still in Sannerz joined

Healed and redeemed, to the Spirit give thanks.
Torn out of the dark, join the fight and close ranks.
Whate'er was divided shall now be made one.
The three-in-one God shall repudiate none.

For now we have seen it: the Spirit is here.
Demons are scattering, the kingdom is near.
The dark is retreating, night's fleeing in haste.
By signs of God's closeness, devils are chased.

Arise, man of God, then, and go into death.
Let your frail ship be guided by unity's breath,
for great numbers are daring, though blown
   by the storm
that fills its tall sails, toward night to be borne.

On those still divided, Lord, lay thou thy hands.
Quicken the hearts that are freed from dark bands.
Smoke rises upward, and flames blaze and scorch,
the wreckage decaying – but forward the torch!

Rhön Bruderhof, early 1928

We are so base and rotten –
so often we withstand
the Spirit, though its storm winds
blow round our little band.

Defiant, stubborn, willful,
we shut out its holy call,

them. Eberhard was relieved that the long-split brotherhood was finally gathered in one place. But as "Healed and redeemed" indicates, unity still had to be fought for.

der einig uns will behausen,
alle zum Reich verweist.pe

Wir sind so schwach und kläglich,
zu halten Bergeshöh'.
Die schleichenden Feindesmächte
bringen uns Not und Weh.

Wir sind so schwer beweglich
im harten Höhen-Krieg,
verschlafen Entscheidungsnächte,
versäumen heil'gen Sieg.

Du Bergesgeist der Höhen,
komm zu uns, heil'ger Geist!
Du läutest die Sturmesglocke,
die Schar zusammenreisst.

Du ferner Geist der Höhe,
du führst die Schar zum Streit,
dass niemals ihr Schreiten stocke,
sie siege weit und breit.

Wir flehn zum Herrn der Geister,
dass er uns ewig führ'.
Wir rufen den Geistes-Meister:
Weihe die Deinen dir.

Du bist der ew'ge Sieger,
du führst die schwache Schar,
du weihest dir deine Krieger,
taufst sie dir ganz und gar!

Rhönbruderhof, Juni 1928

Despite the tone of this poem, Emmy set it to the tune of

though it points to the kingdom,
there to unite us all.

And yet, too weak and wretched
to hold to the Spirit's heights,
we fall to lurking forces
of need and pain and fright.

So slow to move – to rally
and fight the desperate war,
we sleep through nights of crisis
and miss victorious hours.

Thou spirit of the mountains
come down upon our land!
Ring loud thy storm-bell summons
and muster our fighting band.

Far spirit of the heavens,
lead us into the fight,
that we not flag or falter
but conquer far and wide.

We pray thee, Lord of spirits:
lead us forever on.
O master of spirits, hear us
and consecrate thine own.

Thou art the eternal victor –
lead thou our feeble band.
Baptize us for thy service.
We're thine, at thy command.

Rhön Bruderhof, June 1928

"Der Mönch Waltramus," a ballad about a lovelorn monk.

Nehmt den Geist. Ich gebe ihn.
Nehmt ihn auf und gebt euch hin!
Glaubet nur: ich weihe euch!
Geist ist Feuer, Geist ist Kraft,
Geist bringt Leben, führt ins Reich.
Er ist's, der das Neue schafft.

Nehmt den Geist, die heil'ge Glut.
Er ist's, der die Taten tut.
Glaubt in Treue meinem Geist.
Geist ist Bauen, Geist ist Werk.
Geist ist's, der zur Einheit weist.
Gebt ihm Raum, dass er euch stärk'.

Gebet Raum dem heil'gen Geist,
der das Böse von euch reisst.
Geist ist Wahrheit, ewig gut.
Geist ist Reinheit ew'gen Lichts.
Geist ist Güte, Liebesflut,
Eigenes lässt er dir nichts.

Geist ertötet Blutesglut,
sein Erstreiten niemals ruht.
Geist ist Jahwes heil'ger Krieg,
der den Geist hat hergebracht.
Geist bringt Jesu Kreuz zum Sieg.
Geist ist Siegen heil'ger Macht.

Rhönbruderhof, Juni 1928

In the first verses of "Take the spirit I bestow," the speaker is
God, who calls the church to accept Christ's spirit.

Take the spirit I bestow.
Welcome him, embrace his glow.
Only believe: I hallow you.
The Spirit is fire, the Spirit is might,
he leads to my realm, brings life and light.
He is creator of all things new.

Receive the Spirit's holy blaze:
'tis he who works in you each day,
so trust in him, to him stay true.
He is the spirit of work and deed,
toward unity he points and leads.
Allow him, then, to strengthen you.

Give your heart unto the Spirit,
that he might tear evil from it.
He is light and truth itself.
Like a stream of love that cleanses,
his endless purity and goodness
leave you nothing of yourself.

The Spirit silences and kills
all bloodlust. He is never still.
His fight is Yahweh's holy fight,
a battle he has now made ours.
In him, the cross victorious towers –
and prevails with holy might.

Rhön Bruderhof, June 1928

Wir rufen um die Einheit
den Geist der Liebe an.
Wir bitten um die Reinheit
geeinter klarer Bahn.

Wenn jeder ganz für jeden
im Glauben rufen kann,
wir für einander reden,
wie Abraham getan.

Die Nöte müssen weichen.
Die Lösung naht heran.
Der Geist lässt uns erreichen
die Einheit, Mann für Mann.

Drum, Emmy, lass uns flehen,
das Fürgebet ist stark.
Der Geist will uns durchwehen
Herz, Seele, Leib und Mark.

Wir bleiben eins im Glauben,
ganz nahe, Herz zu Herz.
Der Feind kann uns nicht rauben
Zwei-Einheit – himmelwärts!

Rhönbruderhof, 19. August 1928

Written at a time when Eberhard was actively seeking con-
tact with the Hutterites of North America, this poem reflects
his deep longing for unity with them. So does a letter he wrote
three days later (to Elias Walter of Stand Off Colony, Alberta)

We call upon the spirit
of love to hear our prayer:
give us unity, we plead –
one way, unbroken, clear.

When each one intercedes
for the next, with faith in God –
when each for all can answer
as Abraham did of old –

then will our loads be lifted
and answers be made plain,
and by the Spirit, oneness
shall among all men be gained.

So, Emmy, let us never forget
our strongest weapon, prayer.
The Spirit would cleanse our hearts
and minds and bodies with its air.

Heart to heart united
in faith, we're bound as one.
No foe can ever divide us
on the way that leads to heav'n.

Rhön Bruderhof, August 19, 1928

in which he speaks of the brotherhood's "resolute certainty"
that the Rhön Bruderhof ought to become part of the
Hutterian Church.

Das Dunkle ist vergangen,
die Nacht ist abgetan.
Es schwindet alles Bangen,
der Ängste Alp und Wahn.

Versunken ist die Sünde,
hinabgesenkt in Nacht,
versenkt in dunkle Gründe.
Das Leben ist erwacht.

Die düstre Nacht des Sterbens,
des Leibes Bleigewicht,
der Bann des Fluch-Verderbens
versank im Endgericht.

Dies Richten ist die Güte,
bei Gott ist's völlig eins.
Die Güte uns behüte,
ihr Strahl vernichtet keins.

Die Herzen tief verbunden
schaun wir in Gottes Herz.
Er schlag uns blut'ge Wunden,
er richtet himmelwärts.

Barmherzigkeit im Richten,
Gericht in Gottes Herz!
Der Geist wird alles lichten,
er zündet Kerz um Kerz.

On an early copy of "The darkness has departed," the poem
is followed by a note in Emmy Arnold's handwriting: "Jesus

The darkness has departed,
and night is overcome.
Our nightmares and delusions
and anxieties are gone.

The sting of sin is broken
and robbed of its might,
and drowned in deep darkness –
now life awakes to light.

The gloom of death and dying,
the body's leaden weight,
the accursed thrall of ruin –
the Last Judgment seals their fate.

God's judgment is God's goodness:
in him these two are one.
So may he e'er protect us –
his light will blot out none.

Hearts deeply bound in oneness,
we gaze into God's heart.
Though wounding us until we bleed,
he points us heavenward.

Compassion in his judgment,
and judgment in his love,
he lights each heart – each candle –
with the Spirit from above.

mentions, as the most important things, judgment, compassion,
and faith. All three are one."

Es brennen unsre Flammen
der Morgenröte zu,
die Flammen glühn zusammen,
das Ich versinkt im Du.

Du strahlend Morgensonne,
du zehrst die Flammen auf,
du bist der Gluten Wonne,
du siegst im hohen Lauf.

Das Morgenlicht bringt Leben,
erweckt aus toter Nacht.
Die Kräfte lichtzu streben,
die Sonne hält die Wacht.

Das Dunkle ist vergangen,
die Nacht ist abgetan.
Es schwindet alles Bangen,
der Ängste Alp und Wahn.

Rhönbruderhof, August 1928

Dir muss ich leben, du mein Christus,
so wie du bist und heisst.
Dich muss ich lieben, du mein Jesus,
der du um alle freist.

Dich muss ich halten, du mein Christus,
so wie du heilst und löst.

Eberhard wrote "I must live for you" on the title page of a
New Testament that belonged to Rose Meyer (later Kaiser).

And as our flames flare upward
to meet the rising sun,
each "I" is lost in "thou" –
all fires burn as one.

Thou glorious sun of morning,
engulf our feeble flames!
Across the vault of heaven
thy victory proclaim.

The light of morning wakens
new life, and death must fly.
New energies strive toward the light –
the watching sun on high.

Our nightmares and delusions,
fear, panic – all are gone,
for night is truly vanquished,
and darkness overcome.

Rhön Bruderhof, August 1928

I must live for you, my Christ –
for you, just as you are,
and I must love you, my Jesus.
You seek all, near and far.

I must cling to you, my Christ,
to your healing, saving might,

Dich muss ich schauen, du mein Jesus,
wie du im Kampfe stehst.

Dir muss ich danken, du mein Christus,
wie du zerschlägst, zerbrichst.
Dir muss ich lauschen, meinem Jesus,
so wie du wirkst und sprichst.

Dich muss ich hören, du mein Christus,
wie du uns weckst und rufst.
Dir muss ich glauben, du mein Jesus,
dir, der du alles schufst.

Dir muss ich trauen, du mein Christus,
so wie du nimmst und gibst.
Dir muss ich folgen, du mein Jesus,
so, wie du dienst and liebst.

Dir muss ich arm sein, du mein Christus,
wie du in Armut darbst.
Dir soll ich gleichen, du mein Jesus,
so wie du littst and starbst.

Dich will ich ehren, du mein Christus,
der du allein regierst.
Dein will ich bleiben, du mein König,
dass du nur Herr mir wirst.

Rhönbruderhof, 1928

and I must look to you, who stand
steadfast in every fight.

I must thank you, Christ –
you who chasten with your rod;
and I must hear your voice, my Lord:
you are the word of God.

I must hearken to you, my Christ,
as you arouse and call,
and I must trust in you, Christ Jesus –
you who created all.

I must trust you, Christ,
whether you take or give,
and I must follow you, my Lord.
You serve with endless love.

I must be poor for you, my Christ –
you who were sore deprived,
and I must be like you, my Jesus –
you who suffered and died.

I will sing your praises, Christ,
for you are Lord alone.
I am forever yours, my king –
I kneel before your throne.

Rhön Bruderhof, 1928

Ich weiss ein Land in naher Fern,
es liegt in leerer Flur.
Die Wüste sperrt des Berges Kern,
dort sucht man Goldes Spur.
Der reichste Schatz der weiten Erd'
gehört dem Einheits-Mut.
Gold-Ader-Tiefen nie erhört
verschenken edles Gut.

Der Weg, den dieses Land dir weist,
ist frei nur dem, der frei.
Der frei von aller Habe reist,
liess alles, was es sei!
Das eigne Gut im alten Land,
er gab's der Armen Not.
Der Wille riss das eigne Band,
er tat's um Christi Tod.

Von drüben winkt das neue Reich.
Die Freude wartet sein.
Sie bricht das Alte hart und gleich,
sie tötet Mein und Dein.
Es bleibt der grösste Tor der Erd,
wer hängt am eignen Gut.
Er tappt in Blindheit unerhört,
stürzt tot in eigne Glut.

Im Tode bleibt er fern dem Land,
wo Freuden-Einheit strahlt.
Zu lange blieb ihm unerkannt,
dass Geiz nur Tod bezahlt.

I know a land not far away,
amid the empty fields.
The wilderness hems in its hills,
where seekers dig the yield
of veins whose undreamt depths
hold riches pure and bright:
gold, the treasure of those who have
the courage to unite.

The way to this new country
is there alone for him
who travels without any goods –
who has rid himself of them,
who gave all that he owned
in his old land to those in need,
broke loose from self, for Christ,
who died that he be freed.

This kingdom beckons us to come
and share its simple joys.
There, time-worn ways are shattered,
and "yours" and "mine" destroyed.
There, the greatest fool is he
who clings to his own wealth.
He gropes about in blindness black
and plunges to his death.

Yes, such a man is mired
far from the land of unity
in living death, unwitting
of greed's deathly penalty.

Drum, Brüder, auf zur Bruderschaft!
Gemeinschaft leuchtet auf:
Die Habe sei hinweggerafft,
geeint auf einen Hauf.

Wo keiner mehr im Eigennutz
den eignen Reichtum sucht,
wo Einheit wirkt im Geistesschutz,
bleibt Eigentum verrucht.
Drum lassen wir das eigne Land,
hebt hoch Gemeinschafts-Gut!
Wirkt, schafft und gebt mit fester Hand!
Heil jedem, der es tut!

Rhönbruderhof, 1928

Nun sind wir vereinigt, wir folgen dem Geist.
Nun sind wir gereinigt, der Geist uns jetzt weist.
Wir glauben dem Zuspruch. Wir fühlen den Hauch;
sein Atem gibt Freiheit von Nebel und Rauch.

Der Wind ist gewendet, die Luft ist jetzt klar,
die Stürme sind wehend. Die Wahrheit ist wahr.
Die Flamme ist brennend, die Reinheit ist rein.
Die Adern sind rollend, das Blut strömt wie Wein.

Der Sturm ist am Brausen. Das Feuer ist Strahl.
Der Blutwein gibt strömend das heilige Mahl.
Die Wasser sind flutend, das Bad ist das Grab.
Versenkt wird die Sünde mit all ihrer Hab'.

Der Herr ist erstanden! Das Leben steht auf.
Gerechtigkeit sieget im heiligen Lauf.

So brothers, up to brotherhood –
community's new day –
with all possessions on one heap,
what's private, swept away.

Where no one seeks to build his wealth
or keep a separate purse,
where unity of spirit reigns –
there property's a curse.
So let us leave our private plots,
to share all things anew,
and work and give with willing hand –
hail all those who do!

Rhön Bruderhof, 1928

United at last, we are at last made pure.
We follow the Spirit, whose counsel is sure.
We trust in his promise; we feel his touch.
We're freed by his breath from the fog's
      murky clutch.

The wind is changing. Now the air is clear.
Storm winds are blowing. Truth truly is here,
and purity unbroken, and flames that burn and shine.
Through every vein courses new blood, like wine.

Storm winds toss. The fire roars.
Blood-wine for the holy meal is poured.
The river is rising; its flood the grave
of castaway sin and all that enslaves.

The Lord is arisen. Life revives, and grace.
Justice is victorious in life's holy race.

Die Kräfte erwachen, der Dienst wird getan,
die Arbeit beginnt nun. Wir halten die Bahn.

Nun ist es gekommen: Der Geist wirkt und lebt.
Er bändigt das Chaos, in Kraft es umschwebt.
Der Geist ist am Sprechen, die Seele ihn hört.
Wir horchen und schauen, was Gnade uns lehrt.

Nun ist es geschehen: Der Glaube ist da,
der Wille ist Tat, die Befreiung geschah.
Wo Gott wirkt, ist Glaube, der Glaube ist Tat.
Der Glaube wirkt Liebe, die Liebe weiss Rat.

Rhönbruderhof, 1928

Der heil'ge Geist ist gut und zart,
sein Hauch ist freier Wind.
Ihm trotzt der Menschenwille hart,
der Geist sucht nur das Kind.

Des toten Menschen Widerstand
verscheucht den heil'gen Geist,
wenn Seine aufgehobne Hand
den Höhenweg uns weist.

Der heil'ge Geist naht im Gericht,
er sprüht im Feuermeer.
Die Glut zerschmilzt das Schwergewicht
in Sternen-Wiederkehr.

As he strove for a deeper relationship with the Hutterite
brothers, Eberhard was stirred by their earnest belief in the
power of the Holy Spirit. In a letter to the Anabaptist scholar

New strength awakes for the course to be run.
Stand ready to serve – there's work to be done.

The hour has come: the Spirit is at work.
He masters the chaos, his power asserts.
The Spirit is speaking. The soul hears his voice
and listens, perceiving the teachings of grace.

Now it has happened: we have believed.
Our will's become action; we have been freed.
God works where faith lives, and faith means deeds.
Faith nurtures love, and love counsels our need.

Rhön Bruderhof, 1928

The Holy Spirit's gentle breath
is good and free and mild.
But man's hard will defies his wind,
and so he seeks the child.

Dead men resist the Spirit's call
and scare him from their sight.
Still, his uplifted hand makes clear
the way into the heights.

The Spirit comes as judgment,
as a spitting sea of fire,
melts gravity, and lifts dead weight
amid the circling stars.

John Horsch (September–October 1929), he writes, "Their prayer for the Holy Spirit proves that the truth is still living and active among them, and is not and cannot be extinguished."

Der heil'ge Geist uns Christus bringt.
Im Geist strahlt er uns zu,
dass er als Licht die Herzen dringt.
Sein Strahl bricht ein im Nu.

Der heil'ge Geist macht frei und rein,
die Flut umströmt uns ganz.
Wir trinken seinen starken Wein,
gekrönt mit seinem Kranz.

Der heil'ge Geist zur Höhe führt,
er heisst Gerechtigkeit.
In ihm die Bruderschaft regiert
in Liebe allezeit.

Der heil'ge Geist ist gross und stark,
nur er ist's, der uns eint.
Er fährt als Schwert durch Herz und Mark.
Der Geist die Wahrheit meint.

Rhönbruderhof, 1929

Gott ist die Einheit
in ewiger Reinheit,
Christus die Liebe
in heiligem Triebe!

Sein ist die Sendung
in lichter Vollendung,
Brüdern gegeben
in einigem Leben.

The Holy Spirit brings us Christ –
he gleams into our night
and penetrates at once each heart
on whom he casts his light.

The Spirit makes us free and pure;
his streams flow all around.
We drink his strong and living wine,
with his fresh garlands crowned.

The Spirit leads us upward,
righteousness his holy name.
In him true brotherhood and love
throughout all time shall reign.

The Holy Ghost is great and strong,
'tis he who makes us one.
A sword that pierces heart and bone,
he speaks the truth alone.

Rhön Bruderhof, 1929

God is unity
and endless purity.
Christ's love is alive,
a holy drive.

His is the mission
of shining perfection,
entrusted to brothers
who love one another.

Wir sind die Brüder,
sind's wieder und wieder!
Wir sind die Boten,
wie er uns geboten.

So lebe die Freundschaft
in Geistes-Gemeinschaft,
im heiligen Werke
der liebenden Stärke!

Rhönbruderhof, ca. 1929

So komm, wir reichen dir in Liebe
die Hände ein'ger Bruderschaft.
Uns halten heil'gen Geistes Triebe,
von Herz zu Geist webt Seine Kraft.

Der Bund besteht in Geistesreinheit.
Es ist die Wahrheit unser Band.
Uns hält der heil'gen Liebe Einheit,
es ist Gemeinschaft unser Stand.

So lass den Dienst der toten Staaten,
lass alles, was in Macht besteht.
Stirb ab der Lüge Unkraut-Saaten,
der Kirche, die mit Reichtum geht.

Eberhard presented "Come, take" to the brotherhood as a song on May 27, at the baptism of nine brothers and sisters. Three days later he left Hamburg for North America for what turned out to be a full year away from home. Remembering the occasion in 2002, Gertrud Wegner wrote, "We children did not often come to special events, but this time Eberhard invited us to take part. The brook in the Oberzeller Grund had been

We are these brothers;
this is our goal.
We carry the message
given us of old.

Long live our friendship
in spiritual kinship,
in love's strength, the root
of our holy pursuit!

Rhön Bruderhof, ca. 1929

Come, take the hand of brotherhood
that we extend to you in love,
as guided by the Holy Spirit,
whose strength runs through us from above.

Our covenant is eternal truth,
our bond, the Spirit's purity.
Held together in holy love,
we stand firm in community.

Leave the dead State's service –
leave everything that's built on force.
Kill off the weed-seeds of deceit,
reject the worldly, wealthy church.

dammed up to make it deep enough for immersion, and after
supper we all walked up to that beautiful place in the woods.
Eberhard spoke about baptism…and then baptized each one.
At the end of the meeting we sang this song. I remember feeling that Jesus was right there with us…We went home across
the meadows by the light of flaming torches, our hearts full of
what we had experienced."

EBERHARD ARNOLD | **275**

Sag an den Krieg des heil'gen Geistes
der Sinne Gier, dem Eigentum.
Ja, Bruch dem Reich der Grossen heisst es.
Des Kreuzes Schmach sei nun dein Ruhm.

Du wählst den Tod der Lebensstreiter,
du stirbst, denn du bekriegst den Tod;
so wirst dem Reich du Wegbereiter,
so wird Gemeinschaft, lebst du Gott.

Ins Wasser tauchen ruft zur Busse –
Vergebung, Leben bringt ihr Ruf,
zu folgen Jesus auf dem Fusse,
dem Gott im Grabe Leben schuf.

Lebendig, heilig bleibt sein Leben,
das aus dem Tode auferstand.
Im Welten-Tod wir tief erbeben,
er, der die Tode überwand.

Vom Wassergrabe auferstehen,
das bleibt der Taufe heil'ger Sinn.
Nun mannhaft schreitend, siegend gehen,
das heisst, dem Reich sich geben hin.

Der Arbeitseinheit hingegeben,
in Schaffenseinheit lebt Sein Leib.
Gerechtigkeit heisst hier das Leben,
hier wirkt in Einheit Mann und Weib.

Der Werktat Friede will Gemeinde.
Im Warten rufen, flehen wir.
Die Arbeit eint die Gottesfreunde,
wir öffnen Tür und Tore dir.

Take up the Holy Spirit's war!
Fight lust and greed for property.
Break with the worldly urge for fame –
let cross and shame your glory be.

A fighter for life, you've chosen death,
to conquer it, you are ready to die,
blazing a trail for the kingdom of God –
for his community, here and on high.

The plunge of baptism means repentance –
it calls for forgiveness and new life.
It bids us walk in the steps of Jesus,
whom God raised up amid death's strife.

And that life still is quick and holy,
for it is his who rose from death
and conquered it. And he is with us,
though the world's end takes our breath.

The holy meaning of baptism is
to rise up from the water's grave,
to stride forth, manly and victorious,
yet surrendered to God's reign.

Christ's body lives in work united,
devoted to one task alone.
Here daily life is lived in justice,
here man and woman toil as one.

The church is built by peace in action.
We wait and pray – O hear our plea.
As friends of God in work united,
we open all our doors to thee.

Die stille Seele hört dein Rufen.
Du kommst und nahst, wir spüren Näh'.
Wir werfen uns vor deine Stufen.
Komm, Herr, als Geist im Feuer weh'!

Ja, sende deine Feuersfluten!
Einst war es nur ein Wassergrab.
Du tauchst uns ein in Sonnengluten,
du brennst uns alles Tote ab.

So soll der Geist uns übergiessen,
dein Feuer zehrt und hebt uns auf.
Die Flammen lodern, stürmen, fliessen.
Des Geistes Tauf ist Flammen-Lauf!

Rhönbruderhof, Mai 1930

Aus Kampf und Not,
aus Kreuz und Tod
ward die Gemeine:
In Menschen-Schuld,
in Gottes Huld –
Geist war's alleine.

In Dunkelheit,
in Eigenheit
brach Licht als Klärung
in Blut und Leid!
Gelassenheit
schuf die Bewährung.

Written while Eberhard was in North America visiting the
Hutterites, "Through struggle and loss" reflects his enthusiasm

The quiet soul can hear thy voice
at thy approach, and calls thy name,
and throws itself before thy feet:
come, thou Lord, thou spirit aflame!

Send down on us thy fiery flood,
who yet know but the watery grave.
Immerse us in thy sun's hot embers,
all deadness in us burn away.

Thus shall the Spirit be poured out
and cleanse us with its searing force –
with flames that blaze and storm and flow
in one great fiery baptismal course.

Rhön Bruderhof, May 1930

Through struggle and loss,
death and the cross,
the church arose.
Despite man's guilt,
God's grace was spilled –
his Spirit blows.

Light broke the gloom
of self-love's tomb;
it cleansed and blessed
blood, pain, and distress.
In yieldedness
man stood the test.

at the prospect of joining a church whose history was one of
conviction, missionary zeal, persecution, and martyrdom.

Ja: Christi Ruf
hier Einheit schuf.
Er war der Meister,
dass all' in Ein'
dort werden rein:
Einig die Geister!

Des Feindes Wut,
der Hölle Glut
schlug hoch das Feuer.
Die Sendung kam:
Die Leiber nahm
Leu, Wolf und Geier.

Der Botschaft Trieb,
die reine Lieb
führte die Brüder
wie Lämmer zart.
In Christi Art
wagten sie's wieder.

Die Macht im Staat,
Gewalt im Rat
tötete Leiber.
Der Mörder-Geist
den Mann zerreisst,
auch schwache Weiber!

Der Wahrheit Geist,
der Leben weist,
ward nicht getötet!
Der Zeugen Tod,
Verfolgungsnot,
blutig gerötet,

Yes, Christ's clear call
drew one and all
to him, their Lord.
Thus unified
and purified,
they found accord.

In hellfire's glow
the raging foe
threw wide his maw.
Then mission called:
men went, gave all
to the lion's jaw.

By love spurred
to spread God's word,
forth brothers strode,
lambs to the slaughter.
They did not falter
but trod Christ's road.

Council and state –
powers of hate –
killed all in their path.
No man or woman
was spared the demon,
the murd'rous bloodbath.

Yet through all the strife,
truth pointed to life.
It could not be killed.
The reddening flood
of martyrs' blood –
persecution's yield –

gab Kraft so gross
im schlimmsten Los!
Eins macht's die Brüder.
So siegt der Geist:
Im Tod zumeist
naht Er sich wieder.

Auch unsre Zeit
steht neu bereit –
Sein sind die Zeiten –
dass Gott uns Mut
in neuer Glut
tief wird bereiten.

So sei's denn wahr:
mit Haut und Haar
dir unser Leben,
dir Kraft und Gut,
dir Leib und Blut
so hinzugeben,

dass Wort und Tat,
dass Herz und Rat
dein, Christus, bleibe;
dass Arbeitsmut
und Liebesglut
dir, deinem Leibe

ganz zugehört,
dir ungestört
einig zu leben;
im Kampf und Streit
zum Dienst bereit,
ohne zu beben!

Alberta (Canada), Oktober 1930

gave strength and power
in the darkest of hours;
brought oneness, chased fear.
Thus, whatever befall
us, in death most of all,
the Spirit draws near.

In our time too,
we expect him anew.
His are the ages!
May God us inspire
and set us on fire,
and make us courageous.

Yes, let it be so:
that for you we let go
of life and limb –
our strength, our goods,
our body, our blood,
our goodness, our sins.

To you, Christ our Lord,
we give thought, deed, and word:
make them your own.
May our love, zeal, and work
belong to the church –
to your Body alone.

Let every life,
through battle and strife,
in your sight find favor.
May we not swerve,
but stand ready to serve
and never waver.

Alberta, Canada, October 1930

EBERHARD ARNOLD

Ihr habt mich ausgesendet
in der Gemeinde Einheitsgeist.
Gott hatte Mut gespendet,
dass ich so weit hierher gereist.

Du flehst für meine Schritte.
Ja, unsres Jesu Reich gescheh,
bis ich in eurer Mitte
bei euch um seine Wege fleh!

Du stehst im Heilandswillen,
er ist die reine Heiligkeit.
Er wird das Sehnen stillen,
er macht die Wege klar bereit.

Sein Sinn ist rein erschlossen;
wir wollen trauend gläubig sein.
Ihr bliebet unverdrossen,
ihr standet treu, in Einheit rein.

Ja, Gott hat euch gehalten,
sein' Hand blieb deutlich offenbar.
Kein Zwist hat euch gespalten.
Kraftmächte reichte Gott euch dar.

Die Sache dieser Sendung
kann nur die Geist-Bewegung sein.
Gott selbst betreibt die Wendung,
dass die Gefässe werden rein.

In a letter (August 7, 1930) to a fellow Hutterite minister, Joseph Stahl gives a good picture of Eberhard at the time this poem was written: "It is beyond description what joy and inspiration the man finds in our forefathers' writings. It puts us to

United in the spirit
of the church, you sent me out,
and God has led me onward –
upheld, encouraged me throughout.

So pray my steps are guided –
that Jesus' heavenly kingdom come –
until, once more together,
we pray again, "Lord, lead us on."

Stand firm within his will,
who is purity and holiness.
He'll answer every longing,
and he'll prepare the way for us.

And let us trust his purpose –
'tis plain and clear for all to see –
as you've remained till now,
undeterred, in loyalty.

Yes, God's held you together,
his guiding hand is manifest.
No discord can divide you,
whom God with mighty powers has blest.

The movement of the Spirit
is the sole cause of this mission –
that God himself work change,
clean each vessel, and bring fruition.

shame… Arnold seems to me like a second Jakob Hutter, especially in his opposition to greed and to having one's own private property in the community."

So bittest du beständig,
dass uns sein Geist stets bleibe nah,
sein Werkzeug bleibe händig,
Taten geschehen hier und da!

Oh, dass doch seine Kräfte,
der reinen Liebe Feuers-Glut,
des Gotteslebens Säfte
den trägen Geistern gebe Mut!

Dein ständig' Flehn und Warten
bringt die Erhörung täglich nah.
Oft schon wir beide harrten:
Plötzlich – so war die Gnade da.

So dank ich's ihm für immer,
dass du, die Meine, ihm so dienst.
Uns trennen Meere nimmer;
und alles bleibt nur sein Verdienst.

Alberta (Canada), Oktober 1930

Die dunkle Schar der Zornsgewalt,
sie greift nach Stahl und Waffen.
Sie rollt heran, wie Eis geballt,
der Christen Schrift zu raffen.
Der machtgrosse Staat,
er will sein Primat

On November 12, 1933, a compulsory nationwide plebiscite
was held in Germany in order to give every citizen the chance
to voice support for the *Führer*. (Eberhard was privately warned
that those who did not participate would be considered
enemies of the state.) Unable to give Hitler a vote of confi-

Pray, then, without ceasing,
that the Spirit be never far,
and that we, his tools, be ready
to do his work wherever we are.

Would that the Spirit's powers –
the pure love of God's fiery heart,
the essence of his being –
new zeal to sleepy souls impart!

So watch and pray, untiring,
and know the answer's daily near.
How often have we waited,
and suddenly God's grace appeared.

I'll always thank the Father
that you can serve him in this way.
The ocean cannot part us,
for all we do is to his praise.

Alberta, Canada, October 1930

The powers of wrath and darkness rage
and take up steel and weapons.
Their cohorts' icy mass rolls on,
the truth of Christ to threaten.
The state, with power base,
demands the greatest place,

dence, members of the Bruderhof marked their ballots with a
statement to the effect that their allegiance belonged to another leader – Christ. Four days later, the community was surrounded by the secret police in the first of several raids that
took place over the next four years. The same evening,

vollständig und ganz,
fasst Thron, Altar und Kranz.
Wer wird ihm widerstehen?

Das Gotteslicht bleibt Jesus Christ;
es leuchtet auf als Zeugnis.
Sein Sonnenbanner Liebe ist,
die Einheit sein Ereignis:
Auf Tod und Gedeihn
in kreisrunden Reihn
geschlossen vereint,
umschliesst die Gottsgemeind'
den Feind mit reiner Liebe.

Der Kampf entbricht im Flammenbrand;
es sprühen Glut und Funken.
Es lichtet weit von Land zu Land
ein Stern, der nie gesunken.
In weit grossem Streit
entbrennt Christi Leid.
Gott lebt und gibt Licht.
Es nahet sein Gericht,
das grösseste Erleben!

Nur glühend Licht ist Gottes Herz,
das Grösste bleibt die Liebe.
Es liebt Gemeinde himmelwärts,
bleibt frei dem Geistestriebe.
Kein Zwang, kein Gebot,
kein Druck und kein Tod,

Eberhard presented the brotherhood with this poem, which
they sang around his bed (he had slipped and broken his leg a
few weeks earlier) to the tune of "A mighty fortress is our

would totally enthrall,
grasp altar, throne, and all.
Who dares to stand against this force?

The light of God is Jesus Christ,
as witness it shines out afar.
His flaming banner is his love,
and unity, his guiding star.
In life or death close-bound,
linked firm in circle round,
the church of God, made bold,
confronts the foe of old:
love's pure fire now encircles him.

The fight breaks out, a burning brand
that scatters sparks and embers.
Its light spreads far from land to land,
an eye that never slumbers.
Christ's agonies ignite
the world in fiercest fight.
God casts his judging light
on all with saving might.
No greater hour can man befall.

God's heart glows with the purest light –
his love, of all is greatest.
And heavenward drawn by love, the church
is freed to serve the Spirit.
Persuasion is in vain.
No suffering, death, or pain,

God." The original is marked, "A song of the fighting church…
dedicated to our housemother and all the brothers, sisters, and
children in her care."

kein Raub der guten Kind'
von Haus und Hofgesind
kann Christi Geist vertreiben.

Die Bruderschaft mag hassen nicht,
sie hält den Feind in Ehren.
Sie schaut ihm frei ins Angesicht,
sie will die Liebe mehren.
Kein Kriegsdienst, keine Wahl,
kein staatlich Götzenmal,
nicht Macht, nicht Gewalt,
nicht gleissend Missgestalt
soll Christi Bild zerstören.

Im freien Zug bricht auf die Schar
in Einheit, Kraft und Friede.
Sie zieht dahin, der Güter bar,
singt Gott in frohem Liede.
Erneuerter Bund
geschichtlicher Stund,
du Beispiel der Not
dem Zukunftsreich in Gott,
du ehrest Gott ohn'gleichen.

Rhönbruderhof, 16. November 1933

Liebe Emmy, lass uns glauben
dem Kinde Jesus, das uns heilt.
Keine Schwäche darf uns rauben,
dass unser Jesus bei uns weilt.

Dedicated "to my Emmy, in the most serious Christmas-
time we have ever experienced," this poem was written by
Eberhard as he lay bedridden, at a time when every week

no threat to snatch a child
from home and loved ones mild
can drive away Christ's spirit.

Our brotherhood can never hate,
but even respects the foe
and faces him, upright and free,
and longs that love may grow.
No vote, no call to hate,
no idolatry of state,
no violence or force,
smooth lying that distorts,
shall e'er destroy Christ's image true.

So marching on with joyful stride,
in poverty rejoicing,
our strong, united band, at peace,
glad praise to God is voicing.
Our covenant, renewed,
in this dark hour has proved
the world's most urgent need
for God's reign to proceed –
it honors God, our Lord and King.

Rhön Bruderhof, November 16, 1933

Dear Emmy, let us always trust
the Christ Child's healing power.
Despite our weakness, none can take
him from us. He is ours.

brought new worries about the increasing scrutiny with which
the Bruderhof was being watched by the Nazis.

Liebe Emmy, ihn wir lieben,
wie immer, heute, alle Zeit.
Wie er immer treu geblieben,
auch jetzt begleite uns erneut
Liebeskraft der Christusgnaden,
die nimmer weichet, alles gibt:
Kreuz des Christus tilgt den Schaden –
im Tod erbleichet, der uns liebt.

Liebe Emmy, das Vergeben
bleibt doch das eine, das uns eint.
So nur halten wir das Leben,
meins wie das deine, hart beweint.

Liebe Emmy, komm und lieb es,
gebrochnes Leben krank und scheu!
Liebe Emmy, komm vergib es,
der Schuld Verweben täglich neu.

Liebe Emmy, uns zu tragen,
wie schwach auch beide mögen sein,
braucht die Kräfte, die es wagen,
tiefernst im Leide, mein und dein
Leben tapfer hinzugeben
in Krankheitsnöten – in der Not,
die nun alle lässt erbeben,
die Schmerzerhöhten führt zum Tod.

Liebe Emmy, unser Sehnen
entflamm' dem Reiche, das uns naht!
Lass auf Christus fest uns lehnen –
der Drache weiche Gottes Saat!

Rhönbruderhof, Dezember 1933

Dear Emmy, let us always love him:
today, tomorrow – all time through.
He's always stayed by us, kept faith.
May he lead each day anew.
Love's energy – Christ's mercy –
never fails, but freely flows
from him whose cross erased our debts,
through death's darkest throes.

Dear Emmy, in forgiving
lies our only hope for unity.
Only with the bitterest tears
will new life come for you and me.

Dear Emmy, come, embrace it:
a broken life – unsteady, sick.
Forgive the tangled web of guilt
that each new day brings to the weak.

Dear Emmy, let us dare,
no matter how frail or weak we are,
to bear, however great, the suffering
that for each may be in store –
to bravely give our lives when ill,
or when pain gives us no relief,
for that which makes us tremble now
will lead through death those cleansed by grief.

Then, Emmy, let our hope flare up
toward the coming kingdom's day,
and lean on God's own son, to whom
the Dragon himself must soon give way.

Rhön Bruderhof, December 1933

Strahlende Flamme
bringt Feuer und Tod,
heisses Verbrennen
in glühender Not!
Jesu, dir sterben,
Jesu, dir folgen
in Armut und Nichts,
feurig versinken
im Blitz des Gerichts.

Lösung der Bindung
im Strom des Geschehns.
Wendung der Winde
des heiligen Weh'ns!
Strom der Bewegung –
heilige Regung
der kommenden Welt,
Freude der Einheit,
du Geist, der uns hält!

Rhönbruderhof, 1933

Herzen erschlossenes ewiges Wort,
Sohn der Jungfrau, im heiligen Geist,
inwendig bindend Ost, West, Süden und Nord,
neue Schöpfung dich einiglich preist!

Glut der Liebe im strahlenden Licht,
Gottesreich bringend der Erde in Not,

The poem "Brilliant flame" was found in the Rhön Bruderhof nightwatchman's book in 1933. "Eternal Word" was found

Brilliant flame
of fire and death,
consuming blaze
of searing distress!
Jesus, to die for thee,
Jesus, to follow thee
in poverty and nothingness –
when laid low by lightning's
judging fire!

Freedom from bondage
to life's onward flow.
A change in the winds
by your holy breath blown.
River of motion
stirred by devotion –
by the world to come –
Spirit who holds us:
thou art unity's joy!

Rhön Bruderhof, 1933

Eternal Word to our hearts shown forth –
Son of the Virgin, through the Spirit: O Lord,
thou unitest East, West, South, and North.
Thy new creation sings praise with one accord.

Fire-glow of love and radiant light:
bring down thy kingdom to our world of strife.

in May 1936, among papers from Eberhard's manuscript for
"The Living Word," the last chapter of his book *Inner Land*.

ewige Wahrheit! Entweiche uns nicht,
halte uns einig in Leben und Tod!

Rhönbruderhof, 1934

Feuergemeinschaft der glühenden Reinheit –
Lebensgemeinschaft der strahlenden Einheit –
Friedensgemeinschaft der leuchtenden Gluten –
Kreuzesgemeinschaft der taufenden Fluten –
Christus: nur du bist sammelndes Licht!

ohne Datum

Gebet

Herr, du mein Einziger!
Ich bin jetzt dein –
dein für ewig.
Du bist jetzt mein –
du bist der Starke,
du bist der Liebe,
du bist der Einzige,
du bist der Geist. Amen.

Herr, du mein Erlöser!
Du bist mein Tod.
In dir vergehe ich,
in dir versinke ich,
in dir bleibe ich tot.

"Communion of fire" was found among the papers of Hella Headland after her death at Woodcrest in 1972.

Truth everlasting! O leave us not –
keep us united in death, as in life.

Rhön Bruderhof, 1934

Communion of fire, in ardent purity –
communion of life, of radiant unity –
communion of peace: a luminous gleam –
of the cross, in a baptismal stream:
Christ, thou alone art the gathering light!

undated

Prayer

Lord, my only Lord!
I am yours, now
and forever;
and you are mine.
You are strength,
you are love,
you alone
are the Spirit. Amen.

Lord, my redeemer,
you are my death.
In you I perish,
in you I lose myself,
in you I stay dead.

The poem "Prayer" was found among Eberhard's papers in
June 1973 by his eldest son, Hardy.

In dir erstehe ich,
in dir wehe ich,
in dir webe ich,
in dir bin ich erstanden,
in dir lebe ich. Amen.

Herr, nur deine Liebe erlöst.
Deine Liebe ist ewig,
denn deine Liebe ist rein.
Deine Liebe ist gütig,
denn deine Liebe ist Gott.
In deiner Liebe bade ich mich,
in deiner Liebe stärke ich mich,
in deiner Liebe bleibe ich frei. Amen.

Herr, du bist Geist.
In dir bin ich lebendig.
Du bist schöpferisch,
in dir handle ich.
Du bist absolut,
in dir lebe ich,
ohne beengt zu sein.
In dir liebe ich,
ohne beschränkt zu sein.
In dir wirke ich,
ohne Knecht zu sein.
In dir bin ich Herr.
In dir bin ich Geist.
In dir bin ich Kraft. Amen.

Herr, du bist Vergebung –
in dir bin ich rein.
Du starbst für mich,

In you I arise,
in you I breathe,
in you I move,
in you I am resurrected –
in you I live. Amen.

Lord, your love alone redeems.
Your love is everlasting,
for your love is pure.
Your love is kind,
for your love is God.
In your love I cleanse myself.
In your love I strengthen myself.
In your love I remain free. Amen.

Lord, you are spirit.
In you I am alive.
You are creative;
in you I act.
You are absolute.
In you I live
without being confined.
In you I love
without being restricted.
In you I labor
without being enslaved.
In you I am master.
In you I am spirit.
In you I am strength. Amen.

Lord, you are forgiveness –
in you I am pure.
You died for me.

EBERHARD ARNOLD

du warbst für mich,
du bist mein Leben.
In dir ist alles versenkt,
versunken in deinem Tod.
In dir ist alles geschenkt,
in dir bin ich in Gott. Amen.

ohne Datum

Es ist vollbracht.
Er leidet und dürstet.
Er leidet die Gottverlassenheit.
Er übergibt dem Vater
seinen Geist.
Er vereinigt seine Freunde.
Er vergibt seinen Feinden.
Er schenkt dem Verbrecher
seine ewige Gemeinschaft.

Deine Erlösung wird meine Erlösung.
Dein Tod wird mein Tod.
Dein Blut wird mein Blut.
Dein Leib wird mein Leib.

Deine Seele wird meine Seele.
Dein Geist wird mein Geist.
Dein Kampf wird mein Kampf.
Deine Kraft wird meine Kraft.

Early copies of "It is finished" are marked with this note: "The legacy of our Word leader Eberhard, found [in his Bible] after his death and read aloud as a most powerful witness to

You sought me out.
You are my life.
In you, all is submerged –
covered by your death –
and all is freely given.
In you, I am in God. Amen.

undated

It is finished.
He suffers and thirsts –
he is godforsaken.
He commends his spirit
unto the Father.
He unites his friends,
he forgives his enemies,
he accepts the thief
into his fellowship eternal.

Thy redemption shall be mine,
thy death shall be my death.
Thy blood shall be my blood,
and thy body, my body –

thy soul shall be my soul,
thy spirit, my spirit.
Thy fight shall be my fight,
thy strength, my strength.

Christ on November 25, 1935, the day his body was laid to rest
until the day of resurrection."

EBERHARD ARNOLD

Dein Sieg wird mein Sieg.
Dein Leben wird mein Leben.
Deine Reinheit wird meine Reinheit.
Deine Liebe wird meine Liebe.

Deine Sache wird meine Sache.
Deine Wahrheit wird meine Wahrheit.
Dein Opfer wird mein Opfer.
Dein Auferstehen wird mein Auferstehen.

Dein Reich wird mein Alles.

Gott is meine Kraft. Jesus ist meine Kraft.
Der heilige Geist ist meine Kraft.

Du bist meine Kraft gut zu sein.
Du bist meine Kraft zur Arbeits-Leistung.
Du bist meine Kraft zum öffentlichen Kampf.
Du bist so meine Kraft, dass ich keine andere
Belebung und keine andere Beruhigung brauche.

Du bist die Kraft, so für alle da zu sein,
wie Du für alle da bist.

Ich bin gerichtet. Ich bin gerettet.
Ich bin geheilt. Ich bin gesandt.

ohne Datum

Thy victory shall be my victory,
thy life, my life.
Thy purity shall be my purity,
thy love, my love.

Thy cause shall be my cause,
thy truth, my truth.
Thy sacrifice shall be my sacrifice,
thy resurrection, my own.

Thy kingdom shall be my all in all.

God is my strength. Jesus is my strength.
The Holy Spirit is my strength:

Thou art my strength to do any good,
thou art my strength to work and achieve,
thou art my strength on the barricades.
Thou art my strength, that I need no other
quickening, and no other consolation.

Thou art my strength to be there for all,
as thou art always there for all.

I am judged. I am saved.
I am healed. I am sent.

undated

Und haben uns nicht Ihm genaht

Nun muß ich hier so ganz vergeh

Wer kann ... besteh

Er will m... haben,

Verschont ... nicht

Er hat un... laden

Und spra... Leute sp...

Gib mir, ... ganzer H...

Hier ist nur eitel Gram und Schmer...

Drum wollen ... viel Früchte b...

...Ihm für Seine Lieb und Treu

zu danken. Und in allen Dingen

Ihm Dienen, wo und wann es sei

Dann werden wir sehr glücklich sein

Emmy

Herr, nimm dich deines Schäfleins an,
da es sich heut verirrte,
und zeige mir die rechte Bahn,
du treuer, guter Hirte.
Herr, tu' es doch, solange noch
du deine Zeit mir gibest
und mich beständig liebest!

Du halfst mir aus so mancher Not,
die mich schon hat betroffen.
Drum kann ich stets, o lieber Gott,
auf dich auch weiter hoffen.
Du gabest mir, was ich hab' hier
in diesem Erdenleben,
und willst mir noch mehr geben.

Ein reines Herz, das bitt' ich dich,
wollst du, o Gott, mir geben.
Ich möchte gerne ewiglich
mit dir im Himmel leben.
Drum mach mich rein,
dann bin ich dein,
und dann werd' ich dich schauen
auf immergrünen Auen!

Halle, 1899

Also hat Gott uns treu geliebet,
dass er in diese sünd'ge Welt
sein'n einz'gen Sohn selbst für uns gibet

Emmy was fourteen when she wrote this poem. In 1907, at
Eberhard's request, she sent it to him with the next four poems.

Accept this little lamb, I pray,
though it has strayed and wandered.
Show me thy straight path today,
thou good and faithful Shepherd.
O let me share thy tender care
while thou dost give me time
and thy firm love is nigh.

Thy help is always near to me
even when I am disheartened.
Thus shall my hope and faith, O God,
in thee forever be anchored.
Thou'st given me all that I need
in this life here below
and willst yet more bestow.

I ask, dear Father, that in me
a pure heart might be given.
I long in all eternity
to live with thee in heaven.
O cleanse me, so that one day I
might see thee and be healed
and walk on thy green fields.

Halle, 1899

So truly did God love us all
that into this poor world he sent
his own beloved Son to walk

The original of "So truly did God" is marked "after a sermon." Emmy was fifteen when she wrote it.

und uns den Sündern dargestellt,
auf dass die, so ihm hier vertraun,
im Himmel ihn auf ewig schaun.

Er will uns ja auch alles geben,
wenn wir auf seine Güte baun.
Er ist der Weinstock, wir die Reben,
wir müssen ihm nur ganz vertraun
und bei ihm bleiben allezeit,
hier und dort in der Ewigkeit.

Er hat in seinem Wort gesprochen:
„Bleibt meine Jünger früh und spat."
Wir haben ihm das Wort gebrochen
und haben uns nicht ihm genaht.
Nun muss ich hier so ganz vergehn –
wer kann denn so vor ihm bestehn?

Er will mein ganzes Herze haben,
verschont des eignen Lebens nicht.
Er hat uns oft schon eingeladen
und sprach, wie er noch heute spricht:
„Gib mir, mein Sohn, dein ganzes Herz,
hier ist nur eitel Gram und Schmerz."

Drum wollen wir viel Früchte bringen,
um ihm für seine Lieb und Treu
zu danken, und in allen Dingen
ihm dienen, wo und wann es sei.
Dann werden wir sehr glücklich sein
und uns im Himmel mit ihm freun!

Halle, 1900

with us who under sin are bent,
that all who here believe his word
his heavenly glory shall behold.

To those who in his goodness trust,
all that they need he will bestow.
He is the vine, we each a branch.
He only asks that here below
we look to him, wherever we be –
yes, here and in eternity.

In Holy Writ God pleads with us
his true disciples to remain.
Yet we so quickly break our word –
the promises we make are vain.
So am I, too, by shame brought low.
How can I stand before his throne?

He who his own life did not spare
asks for my whole heart as his own.
How many times his call we hear,
to follow him and him alone:
"My child, give your whole heart to me –
on earth is naught but pain and grief."

So let us bear good fruit for him
and serve him at his beck and call
to thank him for the faithful care
that he in love imparts to all.
Then will our hearts with gladness brim
as we rejoice in heaven with him.

Halle, 1900

I.

Der Atem fliegt, die Lippen brennen heiss,
der Puls geht schnell, und schon der kalte Schweiss.
Ich merk es wohl, jedoch ich kann's nicht glauben:
Mein'n Liebling sollt' der Tod mir rauben?

Noch einen Kuss, nur noch 'nen einz'gen Blick,
ein Händedruck im letzten Augenblick.
Und doch, mein Kind, dein Aug' schon
   Schönres sieht,
es sieht ja schon das Glück, das dort dir blüht;
den Hirt, der dorten seine Schäflein weidet
und sorgt, dass auch kein einz'ges Mangel leidet.

Drum zieh nur hin! Ob auch mein Aug'
   hier weinet,
bald kommt der Tag, der uns auf's neu' vereinet.
Dann trennt uns nichts mehr, weder Not noch Tod,
und wir sind oben bei dem lieben Gott!
Vergiss mich nicht, dort in des Himmels Höhn!
Wie freuen wir uns schon aufs Wiedersehn!

II.

Nun hab' ich das kleine Engelein
gebettet in dem weissen Schrein.
Ihr Püppchen sie noch im Ärmchen hält.
Damit spielt sie vielleicht im Himmelszelt,

Emmy wrote these poems after the death of Frieda, a two-
year-old girl she had been caring for in the Halle Deaconess
House, where she was a nurse-apprentice. From her memoirs:

I.

Fast comes her breath, her lips are burning up,
her pulse is racing, cold the drops of sweat.
I see it coming, yet believe it not –
my darling, snatched from me by cruel death?

One final loving gaze, and one more kiss,
hands clasped to hold her from the precipice.
Dear child, do you already see the fair
wide fields of bliss that must await you there,
the loving Shepherd who tends his flock,
and sees that not a single lamb is lost?

Go then to God, my child, though I shed tears.
The day we meet again will soon be here.
Then no more kept apart by death or harm,
we'll be in heaven, in God's loving arms.
Forget me not above in heaven's domain.
How great our joy, when we shall meet again!

II.

And now I've placed my angel here,
all clad in white, upon her bier.
Her tiny arms still hold her precious doll
perhaps to play with in a heavenly hall,

"Death, which often came to the children, pierced me to the heart. I loved one little girl, Frieda, especially. She had one operation after another and died in agony after losing weight for days."

EMMY ARNOLD | 311

wenn sie mit den lieben Engelein singt,
was Gott dem Herrn zu Ehren klingt.
Jeden Abend leuchtet ein Sternlein hernieder,
das winkt mir zu, und tröstet mich wieder!

Halle, 30. April 1903

An Grete

Ich hatt' eine Schwester auf Erden,
die ging zum lieben Gott.
Sie wollt' ein Engelein werden.
Für uns war's bittrer Tod.

Es war mir das Liebste von allen,
sie war so fromm und rein.
Sie flog zu des Himmels Hallen,
sie wollte beim Heiland sein.

Nun spielt sie mit allen den Englein,
die dort bei Jesus sind.
Ich glaube, ich werde nie dort sein,
denn ich bin voller Sünd'!

Halle, 1903

Emmy's younger sister Margaretha, or "Grete," died of appendicitis on October 12, 1903, at the age of fourteen. Her death affected Emmy profoundly. From her memoirs: "After that, I de-

while with her angel-playmates in accord,
she sings glad songs to praise her Lord.
And now a star shines down to me each night
to greet me and give comfort with its light.

Halle, April 30, 1903

To Grete

I had a dear sister on earth
who journeyed to God on high.
She longed to be one of his angels –
still, her death was a bitter goodbye.

I loved her best of all –
so pure and devout was she.
She flew up to heaven's fair mansions,
she yearned with her Savior to be.

And now she is happily playing
with the angels around our dear Lord,
where I fear I may never join her –
I'm too sinful to enter heaven's door.

Halle, 1903

cided that I *had* to find a deeper purpose for my life. I couldn't
stand the thought of remaining at home with my sisters – just
another daughter in another middle-class family."

Nun hast du mich überwunden:
Mein Leben sei völlig für dich!
Laut schall' es: ich bin nun entbunden.
Der Heiland errettete mich!

Er hat schon alles vollbracht!
Ich brauch' selbst nichts mehr zu tun.
Dir folgen bei Tag und in Nacht
bleib' einzig mein treues Bemühn.

Halle, vor Juli 1907

I. Nur Gnade!

Nur Gnade ist's, dass wir ihm folgen dürfen.
Nur Gnade, dass wir ewig Sein!
Und wenn wir hier auch Schweres leiden müssen,
nur Gnade ist es, dass der Himmel mein!

Nur Gnade, dass er uns zusammenführte,
dass wir auf ewig völlig Sein!
In ihm verbunden, unser treuer Hirte
führt uns durch grüne Auen, Dorn'n und Stein'!

Und wenn die ganze Welt uns noch wird hassen,
er hat gesagt: „Sei nur getrost!
Wer Vater, Mutter, alles wird verlassen,
dem geb' ich hier schon mehr: er ist erlöst!"

After Eberhard and Emmy's engagement in April 1907,
relations with her parents slid quickly downhill, in particular
because of the young couple's enthusiastic participation in the
Halle revival. In the fall, on Eberhard's advice, Emmy left home

O'erpowered by your love at last,
I give my life to you: 'tis yours.
Let it ring out that I am free –
the Savior's cut away my cords!

Yes, he's perfected everything –
I need not strive in my own might.
My only goal's to follow you
where'er you lead me, day or night.

Halle, before July 1907

I. Pure grace

'Tis grace alone that we may follow God,
pure grace that we are always his.
And if we bear earth's hardships here,
heaven is still ours: what grace and bliss!

'Tis grace alone that he led us together,
that we might eternally be his alone.
United in him, our faithful shepherd,
he'll lead through pasture, thorn, and stone.

And though the world may look on us with scorn,
he says, "Be comforted! Be not afraid!
Who leaves father and mother for my sake
shall receive yet more: he shall be saved."

and moved to nearby Brumby, where she worked as a children's nurse for a pastor she knew. Emmy loved the children,
but disliked life at the parsonage.

II. Meinem einziggeliebten Ebbo

Und wenn ich droben einst den Herrn werd' sehen
in seiner Schöne, Macht und Herrlichkeit,
dann woll'n wir jubelnd ihm entgegengehen,
ihm danken hier für diese Prüfungszeit,
für seine Gnade und das ew'ge Leben,
für Freud und Leid auf unserm Pilgerpfad,
und dass er, über Bitten und Verstehen,
in dir mein Leben so gesegnet hat!

Brumby, 11. November 1907

Heut zu dieser Sonnenwende
zünden wir ein Feuer an,
wenn auch Sturm und Regenwolken
immer ziehn aufs neu' heran.

Refrain:
Immer heller, immer heller
soll es werden um uns her.
Immer heller soll es brennen,
bis zuletzt ein Flammenmeer!

Will das Feuer nicht gleich lodern,
lasst uns nur nicht mutlos sein!
Es wird doch zur Flammensäule,
wenn der Wind erst zieht hinein.

Inspired by a Reichslied ("kingdom song") from the revival
movement, Emmy wrote these verses for the first anniversary
of the founding of Sannerz, June 21. For a birthday version, also

II. To Ebbo, my only love

And should I at last see the Lord in heaven,
in his splendor, his power, and his majesty,
then shall I go forth with elation to meet him
and thank him for how he has tested me:
for the joys and sorrows of pilgrimage,
for his mercy and grace, for life without end,
for how he, beyond understanding and hope,
great blessings to me through you has sent.

Brumby, November 11, 1907

Celebrate the summer solstice
with a bonfire in the night.
Though it rain, though storm clouds gather,
still the fire must flare up bright.

Refrain:
    Always higher, always brighter,
    Let it burn for all to see.
    Always higher, always brighter,
    Till there is a flaming sea.

If the fire is hard to kindle,
don't lose heart, soon it will grow,
rising like a flaming pillar
as the wind begins to blow.

by Emmy, see *Sing Joyfully*, page 605. For a note about the significance of the summer solstice at Sannerz, see page 344.

Soviel Funken als da sprühen,
soviel Freude wünschen wir,
soviel Leben, Liebe, Friede
ström' uns aus dem Urquell hier.

Sannerz, zum Sonnwendfest 1921

Willst du auf Botschaft gehen?
Ist's nun des Herren Wille,
so will ich in der Stille
derweilen zu ihm flehen,
dass, weil er dich geheissen,
nach Canada zu reisen,
er alles lass geschehn,
was er dadurch ersehn.

Ich gebe dir die Hand,
ich will des Heilands bleiben
und seine Sache treiben
in meinem schwachen Stand.
Du gehest denn schon weiter
und bist sein Wegbereiter
durch Wasser und zu Land.
Sein Sinn ist dir bekannt.

Rhönbruderhof, ohne Datum

Emmy probably wrote this poem in early 1930, as Eberhard
prepared for what turned out to be a year-long sojourn among

Countless glowing sparks soar upward –
may our joys be countless too.
Life and love and peace stream down
from heaven's fount to us below.

Sannerz, summer solstice 1921

If you would bear a message,
and this is God's intent,
I shall not sigh, lament,
but pray for your safe passage.
For if he sends you out
to Canadian shores afar,
will he not then accomplish
his purpose for you there?

I put my hand in yours:
I will the Savior's be,
and further his great cause
despite my frailty.
Go, then: his path prepare,
though far away you fare
o'er water, over land –
he's shown to you his plan.

Rhön Bruderhof, undated

the Hutterites of North America. He left Hamburg for New
York on May 30, 1930.

O heiliger Geist, o ewiger Gott,
lass uns nicht ertrinken in kleinlicher Not!
Wir bitten dich, du Himmelslicht,
du wollst dich von uns wenden nicht.
O heiliger Geist, o ewiger Gott!

O heiliger Geist, o ewiges Weh'n,
du heiliger Wind, du Flamme so schön!
Giess aus auf uns dein's Geistes Flamm',
auf dass wir kommen all zusamm'
zur wahren Gemein, zum ewigen Gott!

O heiliger Geist, o ewiger Gott,
lass unter uns wohnen dein kräftiges Wort!
Des Satans finstres Reich nimm ein,
lass uns schon heute Sieger sein,
vom finsteren Reich zur wahren Gemein!

Rhönbruderhof, Februar 1931

Durch das dunkle Chaos dieses Aeons
tönen dumpfe Klänge des Moderns.
Finstere Mächte durchzittern die Lüfte
und durchbrechen des Todes Ton.
Die ganze Welt steht unter der Herrschaft
dieses mächtigen dunklen Fürsten.

So ist es in den grossen Steinhaufen,
die man Städte nennt.

When Emmy wrote "O Spirit, O God" she had been separated from Eberhard for nine long months. Else, too, was gone,
having been sent by the brotherhood to Switzerland, where it

O Spirit, O God of eternity,
let us not drown in petty need.
We beg thee, heavenly light above,
turn not away from us thy love,
O Spirit, O God of eternity!

O Spirit holy, O infinite air,
thou sacred wind, thou fire fair –
pour out upon us thy great flame,
that we be gathered in thy name
as one true body, in God's own care.

O Holy Spirit, eternal Lord,
dwell with us, thou almighty Word!
And vanquish Satan's dark domain,
that we today the victory gain
o'er darkness, and find thy church again.

Rhön Bruderhof, February 1931

Through the dark chaos of our aeon
ring muffled echoes of decay.
Sinister powers hang in the air,
and mingle with the sound of death.
The mighty prince of darkness
rules over the entire earth.

Not only in the vast heaps of stone
and concrete that people call cities,

was hoped that fresh mountain air might slow her worsening
tuberculosis. (Tragically, it didn't, and she died the next year.)

EMMY ARNOLD

Aber auch in der Natur draussen,
in den felsigen Klüften, in den Bergen und Tälern,
auch dieses Atmen des Todes Gift.
Denn auch dort herrscht dieser Fürst der Finsternis.

Doch da spürt und ahnt man etwas
von der neuen Schöpfung,
die das Dunkle durchbricht.
Sie liegt in den Wehen der neuen Geburt,
um zu erstehen durch des Allgewaltigen Wort,
welches über dem Ringen und Stöhnen
wie eine Vorfrühlingsahnung schwebt.

Wie gelangt nun diese finstere Nacht
zu dem neuen, kommenden Tag?
Gibt es eine Brücke, die hinüberführt
zu dem Sonnensystem der Fixsternwelt,
die nicht gefallen ist in die dunklen Schatten
des mächtigen Todes-Fürsten?
Gibt es einen Weg von hier nach dort?

Die Brücke ist geschlagen!
Der Lebens-Keim des All-Einen Gottes
ist hineingedrungen in dieses dunkle Gebiet
der abgefallenen Schöpfung.
Der höchste Gott sandte seinen Sohn,
geboren von einem Weibe, einer Jungfrau,
die ihr einfältiges Auge gerichtet hatte
auf den Willen des Vaters.

On May 10, 1931, in Bremerhaven, Emmy welcomed Eberhard home from his year in North America with the poem on this (and the next) spread. In it she refers several times to marriage;

but even outdoors, in nature,
in rocky ravines, on peaks, and in vales,
death's poisonous breath is felt, for there too
rules the prince of darkness.

And yet, we can still catch an inkling
of God's new creation, which breaks
    through the dark.
It lies in the painful throes of new birth
and arises at the Almighty's word,
which hovers above all earth's strife and strain
like a foretaste of spring to come.

How will this oppressive night
turn into the light of the coming new day?
Where is the bridge that leads to the sun
with its orbiting planets, and all the fixed stars –
to the world that has never succumbed to the shades
where the prince of death and darkness rules?
Is there a way from here to there?

This bridge has been built!
The life germ of God, who is one and all,
has pierced this dark corner
of fallen creation.
He, the Most High, sent his only son
born of woman – a virgin – who
in simple trust, set her eyes
on the will of the Father.

she was probably thinking of the young couples at the Rhön
who were hoping to marry that summer – though clearly of the
marriage between Christ and the church as well.

Sie, die reine Magd, ein Mensch wie alle Menschen,
nur, dass sie reinen Willens war und ganz demütig
ihren Willen in den des Höchsten legte.
Da wurde durch sie das Wunder,
dass von dem Einigen Gott
der Odem in sie eindrang.

Und sie gebar – nicht durch den Willen des Mannes –
den Sohn, den Erretter, den Fürsten des Lebens,
der Befreiung bringt und einen neuen Tag herauffführt.
Er, der Bezwinger des Todes und der finstren Mächte,
welche noch heute die Erde beherrschen,
soll einst König werden, und dann Alles in Allem.

Seit jener Zeit, wo der Eine
auf dieser Erde wandelte,
ist nun auch in dieser mit dem Tode
ringenden, dunklen Schöpfung
ein Gottes-Funke geblieben,
auch nachdem der Fürst des Lebens,
durch Mörderhand getötet, die Erde verliess.

Er sandte seinen Geist. Und dieser
Geist des Vaters und des Sohnes
wirkt auch heute fort als Licht und als Salz
in denen, die ungeteilten Herzens
sich ihm hingegeben und den neuen Tag erwarten.
Ihr Leben ist symbolhaft und stellt das Ewige dar,
die Einheit, die bei dem Vater war.

In der Einheit zu zweien, die der Höchste schuf,
feiert sie heute die Einheit, die Hochzeit,
hindeutend auf die ewige Hochzeit,

This maiden pure – a woman like others,
though undivided in heart and mind –
humbly bowed and submitted her will
to that of the Almighty God.
Thus, through her, a miracle took place:
the breath of the Holy One entered her.

And so she gave birth – not by man –
to the Son, the Redeemer, the Prince of Life
who liberates us and brings on the new day.
He, conqueror of death and every dark force
that holds sway now – he shall one day be King.
Yes, he shall be All in All.

And since the day God walked the earth,
there has remained a spark divine
in the darkened creation that wrestles with death.
This spark remained after the Prince of Life
met death at the hands of his murderers –
yea, even after he left this earth.

God sent the Spirit of the Father and the Son,
who even now works on as light and salt
in all who give their lives to him
and await his new day with undivided hearts.
Their lives are a symbol of what is eternal:
the oneness the Father has with Christ.

Today we rejoice in the oneness of two,
in the union created by the Most High:
marriage, which points to that great wedding feast,
where a bridge shall be built for eternity

wo die Brücke ewig wird aufgerichtet
zwischen Gott und Mensch;
wo keine Nacht mehr ist und kein Tod
und keine widerstreitenden Mächte,
und keine Trennung mehr ist.

So wartet heute dieser kleine Funke,
die ewige Gottesgemeinde,
auf den Bräutigam, der kommen wird,
ewig Hochzeit zu feiern!
Und so wie durch diese Einheit
zu zweien neues Leben geboren wird,
also wird auch in der Zukunft des ewigen Reiches
beständig neues Leben erzeugt und geboren
durch ihn, der das Leben ist,
und seine ewige Gemeinde.

Rhönbruderhof, zum 10. Mai 1931

An Else

Mir ist es oft, als müsstest herein du kommen,
die du alles mit uns getragen hast.
Wie oft haben wir dich erwartet
und sind dir entgegengegangen,
wenn du heimkehrtest von schwierigsten Fahrten,
die du für das uns anvertraute Werk
unternommen hattest! Es ist mir oft
die Gegenwart wie ein Traum, denn ich lebe
ebenso in der Vergangenheit und in der Zukunft.

Written just one year after her sister Else died (after a
prolonged and agonizing battle with pulmonary tuberculosis)

between God and man; where night is no more,
nor death, nor separation, nor opposing powers.

Already today this tiny spark,
God's eternal community,
awaits the bridegroom, who shall come
to celebrate the great feast without end.

New life springs forth from the oneness of two.
So, too, in God's eternal realm,
new life shall be brought forth without ceasing
through him, who is life,
and through his everlasting church.

Bremerhaven, for May 10, 1931

To Else

Often it seems as if you were
about to enter through the door –
you who bore so much with us.
How many times we waited for you,
or went to meet you as you returned
from the difficult trips that you undertook
for the sake of the task entrusted to us!
Yes, sometimes the present feels like a dream –
I live just as much in the future and the past.

this poem radiates Emmy's love for "the best playmate" of her
childhood and the "lifelong comrade" with whom she shared

Ich sehe dich oft so deutlich vor mir,
als wir beide noch Kinder waren
und gemeinsam teilten Freude und Leid,
wo unser Vater so oft zu uns sagte:
„Es sind sicher wieder Dummheiten,
die ihr euch ausdenkt, wenn ihr so leise die Köpfe
zusammensteckt und euch etwas zuflüstert!"
Wir haben alles miteinander geteilt,
auch unser Suchen und Fragen
nach göttlichen Dingen.

Und als für mich die Entscheidungsstunde
der Berufung schlug, da bist du bald gefolgt
und verliessest unter Schmerzen
und Kummer der Eltern das Vaterhaus.

Ich ging dann mit dem, den Gott mir
zum Lebensgefährten bestimmte.
Und unser Hochzeitstag –
einer der höchsten Tage im Leben –
war dir geteilt, teils Freude, teils Kummer,
denn deine Kindheitsgefährtin
und Jugendkameradin
war durch innerste, göttliche Führung
zur Ehe bestimmt.

Doch bald berief dich Gott,
mit uns gemeinsam zu wandern.

everything. From her memoirs: "Else was cherished by old and
young. There was something of the spirit of St. Francis in her…
Despite her many tasks and her devotion to her work, she always had time for the needs of others, and not only those

At times I see you clearly before me
as you were when we were still children
and shared everything – both laughter and tears.
Father would say, "When it's so quiet –
when your heads are together
and you're whispering –
you can only be planning mischief again!"
Yes, there was nothing that we did not share,
even our seeking in godly things.

And after the hour of decision struck
for me, and my calling was shown to me,
you followed, leaving home as well,
despite the pain it caused our parents.

Then I went with the one whom God
destined to be my life's companion.
At our wedding, a high point of my life,
your heart was torn between joy and grief.
Your childhood companion, your comrade
    through youth
had been guided and led by God into marriage.

But then God called you to walk with us,
and by him, tasks were set before us

within our own ranks. Her trips into the neighborhood and far-
ther afield to beg for help were never without results. Who
could resist this person, so frail in body but so aflame with enthusiasm and love?" For more about Else, see page xii.

Es wurden uns nach göttlicher Weisung
Aufgaben gestellt,
wobei wir dringend der Hilfe bedurften.
Und so arbeitetest du gemeinsam mit uns
in Halle, Tirol und Berlin, bis auf den Tag,
da wir geheissen wurden, aufzubrechen
und in ein unbekanntes Land zu ziehen!

So durften wir gemeinsam mit dir
und andern den Aufbau in Sannerz
und auf dem Rhönbruderhof beginnen.
Die Jahre des Ringens und Kämpfens,
des Bekämpftwerdens und Unterliegens,
der Kraft und des Sieges, des Wanderns
auf der Horizontale, so nahe dem Absturz,
sind nicht spurlos an uns vorübergegangen.

Im besonderen Masse wurden dir
durch göttlichen Beistand Kräfte verliehen.
Du durftest dem Werke Geburtshilfen erweisen
und hast, ohne die Gesundheit zu schonen,
dein Leben dem höchsten Dienst geweiht
bis zur letzten Stunde auf dieser Welt,
die dir geschenkt war.

Wie eine reife Frucht fielst Du vom Baume.
Dein Leben steht uns wie ein abgeschlossenes,
vollendetes Ganzes vor Augen,
denn du warst, ja, du bist eingefügt
in den Tempel, ein Stein neben andern,
der der Bau Gottes ist!

for which we urgently needed your help.
And so you worked side by side with us
in Halle, in Tirol, and in Berlin,
until the day we were commanded
to leave all and set out for the unknown.

Together with you we began to build
community in Sannerz and the Rhön.
Those years of wrestling and struggling –
of opposition and even defeat,
but also strength and victory –
or of plodding along horizontally
right at the brink of the abyss:
they did not pass without leaving their mark.

And through it all, a special measure
of strength was given you by God,
so that with your help
a new venture might be born.
You never considered
the state of your health,
but gave every ounce to the highest cause,
until the last hour given to you.

Like a ripe fruit from a tree you fell,
and now your life stands, one completed whole.
You were – indeed, you still are – a stone
fit among others into the temple,
which is the building of the Lord.

Obgleich wir wissen und glauben,
dass du lebendig wirkst,
wenn auch für diese Zeit gestorben –
warum ist man noch so irdisch gesonnen,
dass man dich in Gedanken sucht
in deiner Arbeit und Hingabe, in dem Kleid,
welches du hier trugst, als du noch hier
unter uns wirktest!

Wie oft bin ich in Gedanken versunken
und meine, du müsstest wiederkommen.
Und man sieht voll Sehnsucht,
im Wachen und Träumen,
deiner Rückkehr entgegen!

Es ist mir oft ein tiefer Schmerz,
dass ich niemals wieder dich so sehen soll,
wie du uns verlassen hast, dein treues Gesicht,
deine liebewarmen Augen.

Als ich so den Gedanken nachging
und nicht verstand, was diese Trennung bedeutet,
wurde mir Antwort aus der anderen,
    göttlichen Welt:
Warum suchest du denn die Lebendige
    bei den Toten?
Ewigkeit bedeutet Erfüllung –
Erfüllung des Lebens, der Arbeit, der Zeit,
und die Worte des Johannes kamen
wieder ins Gedächtnis zurück:
Da wird kein Leid mehr sein und keine Trennung,
denn das Erste ist vergangen!

Yes, we know it – we firmly believe –
that though to us on earth you have died,
you are in truth still active, alive.
Why, then, is my thinking so earthly
that I look for you at your place of work,
or in the dress you used to wear
when you still moved among us here?

How often am I
wrapped up in my thoughts
and – awake or in dreams –
think you will come back
and look forward with longing
to your return!

There is such pain within me, knowing
that I will never see you again
as you were when you went: your loyal face,
and your kind eyes, so warm with love.

But when I let my thoughts wander thus,
not understanding what separation means,
an answer comes from the other world:
"Why seek ye the living among the dead?"

Eternity means fulfillment –
fulfillment of work, of time, of life.
And so the words of John come to mind:
"Then shall sorrow and separation be no more,
for the first things have passed away."

So bitten wir vereint mit dir,
die du voran uns gegangen:
Herr, komme bald und richte dein Reich auf,
und vereine alles, was dir gegeben
und was eingefügt werde in den Leib des Christus,
den Bau der göttlichen Verheissung
    und Bestimmung!

So wartet die Braut des Lammes, hier wie dort,
auf die Erfüllung der Zeiten und Ewigkeiten –
auf die Vollendung des Tempels –
auf den wahren Leib, der nicht durch die
    Trennung
von Gott dem Tode bestimmt,
sondern in der höchsten Einheit
für die Unvergänglichkeit bestimmt ist.

Rhönbruderhof, 8. Januar 1933

Vor dem Abendmahl

Der Ruf zum grossen Abendmahl
ist an uns alle ergangen
und wir sind demselben gefolgt.
Ob wir aber dahin gelangen?

Über uns allen lagert immer wieder
die Finsterkeit, die das ganze Erdreich bedeckt.

In the months after Eberhard's death in November 1935,
Emmy began to sense a shift in the inner life of the community – away from Christ, and toward religious bureaucracy. A
lack of unity distressed her as well, as this poem makes plain. It

    POEMS AND RHYMED PRAYERS

And so we pray, united with you
who have journeyed on ahead:
"O Lord, come soon, and establish thy reign!
Unite all those whose lives are thine,
and fit them into the Body of Christ,
thy temple of promise and destiny!"

Both here and above, the Bride of the Lamb
awaits the completion of the temple –
the fulfillment of time and eternity –
and of the new body, which is not doomed
to die through being separated from God,
but is destined in highest unity
for everlasting life: for eternity.

Rhön Bruderhof, January 8, 1933

Before the Lord's Supper

The call to the great Meal of the Lord
has gone forth to us all,
and we have answered and followed it.
But will we reach our goal?

Again and again, darkness settles on us,
the same darkness that shrouds the whole earth.

was written in reference to a strenuous meeting on Easter Sun-
day (April 21, 1936), when the brotherhood at the Alm
Bruderhof was "held up by various petty details" while preparing for the Lord's Supper.

EMMY ARNOLD

Das haben wir auch in letzter Zeit verspürt.
Trotz der Stimme des Rufers,
die so vernehmlich durch das Leiden und Sterben,
welches unter uns geschah, ertönte,
wurden wir immer wieder in den Alltag verstrickt.

Es waren Hindernisse, erkannte und unerkannte,
die uns immer wieder beengten
und auf unseren kleinen Kreis beschränkten.
Doch nach wirklichem Ringen um die Reinigung
wurde uns immer mehr Befreiung geschenkt.
Es wurden Dinge offenbar – was durch
das Wirken des Geistes unter uns geschah.

Neu ruft nun wieder der Geist der Gemeinde,
um sich zu vereinen mit der Braut
    aller Zeiten und Ewigkeiten
im Abendmahl Gottes, zum Gedächtnis
    des Leidens und Sterbens Christi.

Und wir folgen mit Beben als die Unwürdigen,
nicht Fertigen, die den Geist begehren,
um den Alltag und die Wirtschaft zu meistern,
und um als Bereite den Ruf
    in die Welt hinauszutragen.

Werden wir so das Abendmahl Gottes
    halten können?
Als eine Einheit mit der oberen Schar derer,
    die überwanden,
um dereinst – heute stammelnd – im höheren Chor
das Lied des Lammes zu singen?

Almbruderhof, April 1936

We sensed this when, as in recent weeks,
we were caught up by daily affairs and work,
in spite of the clear, strong voice of the Caller
that rang through the suffering and death in our midst.

Again and again there were hindrances,
some obvious, others unrecognized,
which held us back – and so our thoughts
were to our own little circle confined.
And yet, when we truly struggled for cleansing,
freedom grew and increased again.
Thanks to the Spirit's work among us,
hidden things were revealed and made plain.

Now, once again, the church calls out
to be united with the Bride
of all times and eternities, at the Meal of the Lord,
in memory of how Christ suffered and died.

Trembling, we follow, though unfit and unprepared.
We still desire the Spirit's word
to guide our affairs and master each day
and ready us to carry his call to the world.

Will we be able to meet for the Meal,
one with the hosts who have overcome,
and – though we now stammer – join heaven's choir
on high, to sing the song of the Lamb?

Alm Bruderhof, April 1936

O Liebe, die du den Himmel zerrissest
und zu uns auf diese Erde kamst!
Die Erde ist dunkel und Finsternis deckt uns,
du aber kamst, und all' Not auf dich nahmst.

Wir harren, O Jesu, auf dein Erscheinen.
Zum zweiten Mal kommst du. Wir sehn
   nach dir aus.
Dann werden wir alle mit dir vereinigt,
der Tod überwunden – wir sind dann zu Haus.

Der Trennung Zähren sind überwunden,
es ist nicht mehr Zwei, es ist dann nur: Eins.
Wir sind dann ganz frei, gar nicht mehr gebunden.
O jüngster Tag, es fehlt uns keins!

Der Hölle Pforten sind überwunden,
die Krankheit, die Sünde, des ist nicht mehr.
Wann kommst du, Herr Jesus, zu heilen die Wunden,
die Lieblosigkeit schuf? Wann kommst du, Herr?

Cotswold-Bruderhof, 1938

Found in "the locked book," her private memoirs, this poem
forms part of Emmy's pained reflections on the first years of her

O Love, thou that rent the heavens asunder
to come down to us on a darkened earth,
where blackness of night lies over us all,
to take on thyself all its pain through thy birth.

How we await thy second coming!
How deeply we long for thy promised return,
when, death overcome, we are one with thee
in our true home at last: for this we yearn.

Then parting's tears shall be wiped away,
and all shall be one – not divided, not torn.
At last truly free, we shall no more be bound.
On the Last Day none shall be lost or lorn.

The gates of hell shall not prevail.
All sickness, all sin shall be no more.
When comest thou, Christ, to heal the wounds
of our lovelessness? When comest thou, Lord?

Cotswold Bruderhof, 1938

widowhood – and on the state of a brotherhood that she felt
had lost its first love.

Else

Winter Andacht

Weiss liegt der Schnee,
still ruht der See,
hoch des Waldes Zinnen!
Ernst wird mir zu Sinnen.

Horch! Ein Rufen rauscht:
„Gottes Stimme lauscht!"
Hilf aus unsern Sünden!
Komm, uns Wunder künden!

Sannerz, ca. 1921

In Ächzen und Lechzen
stöhnt Menschheit in Zweiheit
und sucht doch die Einheit,
und wird stets gepackt
von Geistern und Mächten,
die trennen und knechten.
Wann kommt denn die Einheit,
die Weltfrieden schafft?

Zu Schlechten und Knechten
kamst du als der Eine.
Du Meister der Geister
strahlst einigend' Licht.
Im Dunkel der Massen,
in Bosheit und Hassen,

Keenly aware of the cosmic battle between good and evil,
Else often revisited the themes of "Tormented, divided." Speaking from her deathbed several years after she wrote it, she said,
"Our life of brotherhood is something wonderful. I know it

Winter prayer

White lies the snow.
No waters flow.
Treetops tower high,
but my heart, heavy, sighs.

Hark! A call is heard –
"Listen for God's Word."
O save us from sin's cold.
Thy wonders now unfold.

Sannerz, ca. 1921

Tormented, divided,
humanity groans,
thirsting for oneness,
yet held and bound
by spirits and powers
that separate, enslave.
When will the unity
that brings world peace be found?

To earth's oppressed
thou camest as the One,
thou master of spirits,
thou unifying light.
Shine into our darkness,
our malice and our hate.

cannot take place except through struggle and strife…But
when things are difficult, we must keep the faith. We must pray
for the Spirit…and we must always remember that God is the
victor in the end."

du Todesüberwinder,
gib Leben aus Tod!

Wir stehen und flehen
um Geist aus der Höhe,
der in uns gestaltet
die heil'ge Gemein.
Gib lodernde Flammen,
die brennen zusammen
in heilig ew'ger Liebe.
O Herr, komme bald!

Sannerz, 1925

Tag der Sonnenhöhe du,
kurze Nacht der Dunkelheit:
Freudenflamme jauchzt dir zu
und verbrennet Sündenleid.
Schüret das Feuer zusammen,
eint euch im Licht der Flammen,
weiht euch dem heil'gen Namen
des, der Einheit ist.

Brüder trennet Hass und Geld,
Finsternis das Erdreich deckt.
Da kamst du als Licht der Welt
und hast Menschen aufgeweckt
zum Dienst an deinem Reiche –

Celebrated across Europe for centuries as the high point of summer, June 21 had additional meaning for the circle at Sannerz: it was the date on which (in 1920) the Arnolds had finally abandoned the dying metropolis of Berlin, as Eberhard

Thou victor o'er death,
turn our deadness to life.

We stand and plead
the Spirit from the heights
that thy true church
among us might be formed.
Send down thy flames –
burn us, weld us as one
with thy eternal love.
Come soon, O Lord!

Sannerz, 1925

Longest day of sun's bright light,
shortest night of all dark nights!
Flames of joy leap up, burst in,
burn away the suffering of sin.
Come, rake the fire together
in the light, and find your brother,
serving, with one another,
God, who is unity.

Hate and greed divide men all.
Over earth lies night's dark pall.
Yet thou cam'st, the world's true light,
waking men to live aright:
to serve thy kingdom fully,

called it, in search of a new place – the city of God. Else set her
poem to a theme from Beethoven's *Appassionata,* a tune known
and loved throughout Germany.

das Ungerechte weiche,
und dein Geist herrsche hier.
Dein Will' geschieht.

Ew'ger Tag, der niemals end't,
wann kommst du, o ew'ge Sonn'?
Deinen ewigen Frieden send!
Komm, du Stadt der Freud' und Wonn'.
In deines Lichtes Scheine
wird deine Ein Gemeine
scheinen in ew'ger Reine
dir zur Ehr'!

Sannerz, Sonnenwende 1926

Du grosser Gott und Vater,
wir danken dir so sehr,
dass du vor Übel behütet
weit, weit auf Land und Meer,

den du hinausgesendet
in Länder unbekannt.
Du gabst, dass er vollendet,
wozu du ihn gesandt.

Der Geist uns eint in Liebe
in Jakob Hutters Gmein.
Der Geist uns ewig bindet
mit allen Zeugen rein.

Du gabest nun den Auftrag,
zu sammeln deine Schar,

Else sent this poem from Switzerland (see note on page

that injustice give way wholly,
and thy Holy Spirit reign only.
Thy will be done.

O thou never-ending day,
when com'st thou, eternal sun, to stay?
Bring us everlasting peace,
city bright of joy and bliss.
From thee pure radiance streams
as one church, united, gleams.
Its brightness forever streams –
Glory to thee!

Sannerz, summer solstice 1926

Almighty God and Father,
we thank thee from our hearts
for guiding and protecting
o'er land and sea afar

him who was thy envoy
in distant, unknown lands.
Through thee he has completed
the task laid in his hands.

Love's spirit, which unites us
with Jakob Hutter's church,
shall bind us all forever
with each witness to the truth.

Thou gavest us this mission:
to gather all thy souls,

320) to welcome Eberhard home from North America.

dass sie in Einheit lebe
in allem, ganz und gar.
Die Lampen sind bereitet,
um Geistes-Öl wir flehn,
dass wir, wenn du erscheinest,
dir wach entgegengehn!

Fidaz (Schweiz), Mai 1931

Sieben Flammen brennen in dunkler Nacht.
Ein Singen und Klingen so hell und so rein
ein Wandrer hört aus der Ferne.

Sie haben getötet sieb'n Zeugen des Herrn,
O Wehe und Jammer auf dieser Erd,
sie konnten die Wahrheit nicht hören.

Und ew'ge Wahrheit nicht schweigen kann.
In Tod und Leid und in Sündenheit
die Menschheit sonst ewig verderbet.

Das Lied ruft neue Zeugen auf,
die folgen dem Lamme bis in den Tod –
das Lied der Überwinder auf Erden.

Die Flammen brennen fort und fort
und zünden weiter von Ort zu Ort
vom Feuer der ewigen Liebe.

Rhönbruderhof, ohne Datum

Found in Else's New Testament after her death on January
11, 1932, this poem commemorates seven Anabaptists (one of
them a 16-year-old) who were martyred for their faith on
December 7, 1531, in Swabia. According to the Hutterian

that they might live, in every way,
as one united whole.
Our lamps are cleaned and ready,
for the Spirit's oil we plead,
that we at thy return be found
prepared, Lord, thee to greet.

Fidaz, Switzerland, May 1931

Seven flames burn brightly in the night.
From far off a wanderer sees their light
and hears pure, clear voices singing.

They killed seven witnesses of the Lord.
O wretched earth, when truth won't be heard,
when men will not let it be spoken.

Yet eternal truth cannot silent be
or else man would suffer mortally,
in sin would forever perish.

The voices call new witnesses to rise
and follow the Lamb of God, though they die.
Their song is the song of victors.

The flames burn on and never cease,
but kindle new blazes from place to place
with the fire of love eternal.

Rhön Bruderhof, undated

Chronicle, a wayfarer who passed the place of execution at evening saw seven lights and heard singing. When word spread of what he had heard and seen, the city council bribed him into silence.

Index of first lines and titles

Poems marked with a dagger were included in *Sonnenlieder* I (1924) or II (1932). Poems marked with an asterisk can be found (sometimes in abridged form) in *Songs of Light*.